THE
1,350
TOUGHEST
TV
TRIVIA
QUESTIONS
OF ALL TIME

THE
1,350
TOUGHEST
TV
TRIVIA
QUESTIONS
OF ALL TIME

By
Vincent Terrace

A CITADEL PRESS BOOK
Published by Carol Publishing Group

A Citadel Press Book
Published by Carol Publishing Group
Citadel Press is a registered trademark of Carol Communications, Inc.

Editorial, sales and distribution, and rights and permissions
inquiries should be addressed to Carol Publishing Group, 120
Enterprise Avenue, Secaucus, N.J. 07094.

In Canada: Canadian Manda Group, One Atlantic Avenue, Suite 105,
Toronto, Ontario M6K 3E7

Carol Publishing Group books may be purchased in bulk at special
discounts for sales promotion, fund-raising, or educational purposes.
Special editions can be created to specifications. For details, contact:
Special Sales Department, Carol Publishing Group, 120 Enterprise
Avenue, Secaucus, N.J. 07094

Manufactured in the United States of America
10 9 8 7 6 5 4 3 2 1

Library of Congress Cataloging-in-Publication Data

Terrace, Vincent, 1948–
    1350 toughest TV trivia questions of all time / Vincent Terrace.
        p. cm.
    Rev. ed. of: 1201 toughest TV trivia questions of all time. © 1995.
    "A Citadel Press book."
    ISBN 0–8065–2082–5 (pbk.)
    1. Television programs—United States—Miscellanea.   I. Title.
    II. Title: One thousand three hundred fifty toughest TV trivia
    questions of all time.
    PN1992.9.T464   1999
    791.45'75'0973—dc21
                                                            98–53112
                                                                CIP

CONTENTS

INTRODUCTION   xiii

HOW TO USE *1,350 Toughest TV Trivia Questions of All Time*   xiv

Chapter 1: Comedy   1

The Abbott and Costello Show   1
The Addams Family   1
ALF   3
Alice   5
All in the Family   5
Amen   5
The Amos 'n' Andy Show   7
The Andy Griffith Show   7
Angie   9
Anything But Love   9
Baby Talk   11
Bachelor Father   11
Benson   13
Bewitched   13
Blossom   15
Bob   15
The Bob Newhart Show   17
Bosom Buddies   17
The Brady Bunch   19
Bridget Loves Bernie   21
Captain Nice   21
Car 54, Where Are You?   23
Charles in Charge   23
The Charmings   25
Cheers   27
Clarissa Explains It All   29
The Cosby Show   31
Davis Rules   33
Dear John   33
December Bride   35
Delta   35
Designing Women   37
The Dick Van Dyke Show   39
A Different World   41

Diff'rent Strokes   43
Dinosaurs   45
Dobie Gillis   47
The Donna Reed Show   49
The Duck Factory   49
Duffy's Tavern   51
Empty Nest   51
Evening Shade   53
F Troop   55
The Facts of Life   57
Family Matters   59
Family Ties   61
Father Knows Best   63
Flying Blind   63
The Fresh Prince of Bel Air   65
Full House   67
The George Burns and Gracie Allen Show   69
The Ghost and Mrs. Muir   69
Gidget   71
Gilligan's Island   73
Good Times   73
Green Acres   75
Growing Pains   75
Happy Days   77
Hazel   81
Head of the Class   83
Home Improvement   85
The Honeymooners   85
I Love Lucy   87
I Married Joan   89
The Jack Benny Program   91
Just the Ten of Us   91
Kate and Allie   93
Laverne and Shirley   93
Leave It to Beaver   95
Love and War   97
Love That Bob   99
Mad About You   99
Madame's Place   101
Major Dad   101
Mama's Family   103
Married...with Children   105
The Mary Tyler Moore Show   107

M*A*S*H   109
Mork and Mindy   111
Mr. Belvedere   111
The Munsters   113
The Munsters Today   115
Murphy Brown   117
My Living Doll   119
My Mother the Car   119
Newhart   121
Night Court   123
The Odd Couple   125
One Day at a Time   127
Our Miss Brooks   129
Out of This World   129
The Patty Duke Show   131
The People's Choice   133
Perfect Strangers   133
The Phil Silvers Show   135
The Powers That Be   137
Roc   137
Roseanne   139
Seinfeld   139
Silver Spoons   141
The Simpsons   141
Small Wonder   143
Step by Step   145
Taxi   145
That Girl   147
Three's Company   149
The Tony Randall Show   149
Too Close for Comfort   151
227   151
Webster   153
Welcome Back, Kotter   153
What's Happening!!   155
Who's the Boss?   155
WKRP in Cincinnati   157

Chapter 2: Drama and Adventure   159

The A-Team   159
Adventures in Paradise   161
Airwolf   161
The Avengers   163

Banacek   163
Batman   163
Baywatch   165
Beauty and the Beast   167
Beverly Hills, 90210   167
The Bionic Woman   169
B.J. and the Bear   169
Bourbon Street Beat   171
Buck Rogers in the 25th Century   171
Charlie's Angels   173
China Beach   173
CHiPs   175
Civil Wars   177
Columbo   177
The Commish   179
Dark Shadows   179
Doogie Howser, M.D.   181
The Dukes of Hazzard   181
Dynasty   183
Eight is Enough   183
The Fall Guy   185
Family   187
Fantasy Island   187
Father Dowling Mysteries   189
The Flash   189
The Greatest American Hero   191
Hardcastle and McCormick   193
Hart to Hart   193
Hawaiian Eye   193
In the Heat of the Night   195
The Invaders   195
The Islanders   197
Jake and the Fatman   197
Johnny Bago   199
Key West   199
Knight Rider   201
Life Goes On   201
The Love Boat   203
McMillan and Wife   203
Magnum, P.I.   203
Matlock   205
Max Headroom   207
Melrose Place   207
Midnight Caller   207

Moonlighting   209
Murder, She Wrote   209
Naked City   211
Northern Exposure   211
Perry Mason   213
Picket Fences   213
Police Woman   213
Reasonable Doubts   215
Remington Steele   215
Richard Diamond, Private Detective   217
The Roaring 20's   217
Search   219
77 Sunset Strip   219
Silk Stalkings   221
Sisters   221
South Beach   223
Street Hawk   223
SurfSide 6   223
The Waltons   225
Wonder Woman   227

Chapter 3: Kid Shows, Science Fiction Series and Westerns   229

The Adventures of Superboy   229
The Adventures of Superman   229
Alien Nation   231
Andy's Gang   231
Annie Oakley   233
Astro Boy   233
Battlestar Galactica   235
The Beany and Cecil Show   237
The Big Valley   237
Bonanza   237
Branded   239
Bronco   239
Captain Scarlet and the Mysterons   241
Captain Video and His Video Rangers   241
Cheyenne   243
Colt .45   243
Dr. Quinn, Medicine Woman   245
Dudley Do-Right of the Mounties   245
The Eighth Man   245
The Flintstones   247
George of the Jungle   247
The Ghost Busters   249

The Guns of Will Sonnett   249
Have Gun, Will Travel   251
Hotel de Paree   251
Howdy Doody   253
Isis   253
Jeff's Collie   253
The Jetsons   255
Johnny Ringo   255
Land of the Lost   257
Lawman   257
Lost in Space   257
Maverick   259
The Marvel Super Heroes   261
The Mickey Mouse Club   261
The Monroes   263
National Velvet   263
Pistols 'n' Petticoats   263
Planet of the Apes   265
Punky Brewster   265
Quantum Leap   267
Quark   267
Rango   267
Rocky and His Friends   269
Saved by the Bell   269
Sheena, Queen of the Jungle   271
Space 1999   271
Space Rangers   273
Sugarfoot   273
Time Trax   275
Walker, Texas Ranger   275
Yancy Derringer   275
Zorro   277

Bonus 1   277

Chapter 4: Cult Shows   279

Brooklyn Bridge   279
Camp Runamuck   279
Diver Dan   281
Doctor Who   281
Dracula: The Series   283
Eerie, Indiana   283
Forever Knight   285

Forever Knight   285
Harry and the Hendersons   285
M.A.N.T.I.S.   287
The Misfits of Science   287
My So-Called Life   289
Once a Hero   289
seaQuest, DSV   291
The Super Human Samurai Syber Squad   291
Thunder in Paradise   291

Chapter 5: Limited Run Series   295

Bill and Ted's Excellent Adventures   295
Blansky's Beauties   295
Broken Badges   297
Delta House   297
Code Name: Foxfire   299
Double Rush   299
Fast Times   301
Fish Police   301
Get Smart   301
High Sierra Search and Rescue   303
Mann and Machine   303
On the Air   305
Sydney   305
Vinnie and Bobby   307

Chapter 6: Who Replaced Whom?   309

Chapter 7: TV Themes   325

Chapter 8: Bonus Section   341

Chapter 9: 1996–1998   359

INTRODUCTION

TELEVISION EXPERTS TAKE NOTICE. This is not your typical question-and-answer book. It is a butt buster. Sure, you may know that the Munsters lived at 1313 Mockingbird Lane and that Fred and Wilma Flintstone resided in the town of Bedrock. But do you know what Herman Munster's blood pressure was? Or what type of pet Fred and Wilma had? If you do, then this book is right up your alley. If not, you'll be provided with an education in TV trivia that you can't find anyplace else.

No, you won't find questions like "What is the color of 'The Green Hornet's black car" or "On what network does the 'ABC Afterschool Special' air?" You'll find narratives that first provide information on a show, then ask you a question about that show. In a number of cases, the characters to which the question refers provide their own answers.

As you peruse the book you'll notice that the hundreds of series listed here are ones you heard of and saw and, in most cases, remember. Obscure programs and shows are not used here to compile questions. What fun is trying to answer a question on a program you never even heard of? To make for a more interesting book, several questions were used per show rather than using questions from as many different shows, to give you a better chance of answering a number of questions correctly.

So, sit back, put that thinking cap on, and take the challenge by answering *1,350 Toughest TV Trivia Questions of All Time*.

HOW TO USE
1,350 Toughest TV Trivia Questions of All Time

THIS BOOK is divided into nine sections: Comedy; Drama and Adventure; Kid Shows, Science Fiction Series and Westerns; Cult shows; Limited Run Series; Who Replaced Whom?; TV Themes; a Bonus Section; and a chapter on 1996–1998 series. Each section contains questions and answers pertaining to particular shows. Within each section shows are listed in alphabetical order.

For your convenience, the question page always precedes the answer page. Questions are grouped separately from their respective answers. (A "Q" represents a question, while an "A" indicates an answer.)

CHAPTER

1

Comedy

The Abbott and Costello Show
Syndicated, 1952–54

Q1. Bud Abbott and Lou Costello, playing out-of-work comedians seeking employment, lived at the Fields Rooming House at 214 Brookline Avenue. How much a week did they pay in rent?

Q2. To make money, Bud and Lou tried selling hats, roller skates, and "No Peddlers Allowed" signs. They thought they had a chance at the big bucks by going on a TV game show called "Hold That Cuckoo." Lou held that cuckoo (ticking clock) and won the grand prize. What was it?

Q3. Hillary Brooke played a number of roles on the series, including Lou's girlfriend. In one episode she inherited a haunted castle; in another, a ranch in Texas. What was the name of the ranch?

Q4. Although landlord Sidney Fields prohibited pets in his apartment house, Lou had a chimpanzee named Bingo. What did Bingo eat for breakfast?

The Addams Family
ABC, 1964–66

Q5. "Beware of Thing" was posted on the iron gate in front of the Addams house on Cemetery Ridge. Why did the family spell their last name with a second "d"?

I

The Abbott and Costello Show

A1.   Seven dollars

A2.   A box of bubble gum

A3.   The B-Bar-B Ranch

A4.   Watermelon

The Addams Family

A5.   "It distinguishes us from the embarrassingly famous and historic John Adams and family."

The Addams Family *continued*

Q6. Gomez, the nattily-dressed father, was independently wealthy but was also an attorney for the defense. What distinguished him from any other attorney?

Q7. The Addams family had strange tastes. What were the three favorite foods of Gomez and his wife, Morticia?

Q8. Morticia's Uncle Fester once worked as an advice-to-the-lovelorn columnist, and his philosophy was "Shoot 'em in the back." What did he call his rifle?

Q9. Gomez's mother, Grandmama Addams, also resided with the family. What high school did she attend?

ALF
NBC, 1986–90

Q10. ALF was an alien who crashed into the garage of the Tanner Family when the frequencies from Willie Tanner's short-wave radio interfered with those of ALF's space ship. ALF, born on the planet Melmac 229 years ago, craved cats (his favorite meal), and loved to eat. How many stomachs did ALF have and what was his body temperature?

Q11. Melmac was destroyed by an explosion, leaving ALF one of the few remaining survivors. What was the motto of the planet?

Q12. Willie was married to Kate. They tied the knot on July 11, 1967. Where did they honeymoon?

Q13. ALF loved Earth TV and believed cartoons reflected real life. He had two favorite TV shows. One was *Gilligan's Island*; what was the other?

A6. He was responsible for putting more men behind bars than any other lawyer in the U.S.

A7. Fried yak, fried eyes of newt, and barbecued turtle tips

A8. Genevieve

A9. Swamp Town High

ALF

A10. Eight stomachs; 425 degrees

A11. "Are you going to finish that sandwich?"

A12. The Duke of Mist Hotel in Niagara Falls

A13. *Polka Time*

Alice
CBS, 1976–85

Q14. A dish called Mel's Chili was the special of the day (every day) at Mel's Diner, a roadside eatery in Arizona. It was located on which specific highway?

Q15. Alice, Flo, and Vera were the waitresses who constantly complained that they needed a raise. How much an hour did "cheapskate" Mel Sharples pay them?

All in the Family
CBS, 1971–78

Q16. Archie Bunker believed that credit was the American way of life ("That way you can buy anything you can't afford"). Where was Archie first stationed during "The Big One" (World War II)?

Q17. Although he called his wife, Edith, "Dingbat," he loved her very much. Where did Archie meet Edith?

Q18. When Gloria, their daughter, was born in 1944, Edith and Archie could barely afford to pay the hospital bill. How much did Gloria's birth cost?

Q19. In 1948, when TV was new, Archie and Edith couldn't afford a set. Where did they watch *The Milton Berle Show*?

Q20. While Edith never held a regular nine-to-five job after marrying Archie, she did have one prior to meeting him. Where did she work?

Amen
NBC, 1986–91

Q21. Ernest Frye, the deacon of the First Community Church of Philadelphia, also was an attorney. What words appeared on his office door after his name ("Attorney-at-Law Ernest Frye...")?

Alice

A14.   Bush Highway

A15. $2.90

All in the Family

A16.   Fort Riley, Kansas

A17.   At The Puritan Maid Ice Cream Parlor

A18. $131.50

A19.   From the window of Tupperman's Department Store

A20.   The Hercules Plumbing Company

Amen

A21.   "Where Winning is Everything"

Amen *continued*

Q22. Thelma, Ernest's daughter, was called the "Undateable" in high school. What school did she attend?

Q23. Although Thelma could not cook, she hosted a TV show called *Thelma's Kitchen*. What company sponsored it?

The Amos 'n' Andy Show
CBS, 1951–53

Q24. Amos Jones, Andy Brown, and George "Kingfish" Stevens were friends who lived on Lenox Avenue in Manhattan. Amos and Andy resided previously in what Georgia city before "coming up north" to begin new lives?

Q25. Con artist Kingfish sold Andy the cab they used for the Fresh Air Taxi Company of America, Inc. How much did he con out of Andy for it?

Q26. Living by cons was Kingfish's livelihood. What was his favorite activity?

Q27. Sapphire, Kingfish's wife, put up with all of her husband's nonsense. Although they argued constantly, she loved him and was apparently the breadwinner. For what company did Sapphire work?

The Andy Griffith Show
CBS, 1960–68

Q28. Handing out parking tickets and replacing the lids on garbage cans was part of the job for Sheriff Andy Taylor and his deputy, Barney Fife, in the small town of Mayberry, North Carolina. Andy's experiences as sheriff have been written up in the National Sheriff's magazine. What did the magazine call Andy?

Q29. Andy and Barney were actually cousins and 1945 graduates of what high school?

A22. West Holmes High

A23. Bake Rite Flour

The Amos 'n' Andy Show

A24. Marietta

A25. $340

A26. Sleeping

A27. Superfine Brush Company

The Andy Griffith Show

A28. "The Sheriff Without a Gun"

A29. Mayfield Union High

The Andy Griffith Show continued

Q30. Aunt Bee raised Andy and claimed that "Andy is meaner than a bear that backed into a beehive when he doesn't eat supper." Andy was most fond of which of Aunt Bee's desserts?

Q31. Opie, Andy's son, had several pets, including a lizard, a dog, and a parakeet. Dinkie was the parakeet's name, but what did Opie call the dog and lizard?

Angie
ABC, 1979–80

Q32. Angie was a hardworking waitress who found her life turned upside down when she married a rich doctor (Brad Benson). Although Angie did not need to work, she continued to do so in what coffee shop?

Q33. Angie's mother, Theresa Falco, ran the family business, the Falco Newsstand. When a better business opportunity came along, she sold the newsstand and purchased what beauty parlor?

Anything but Love
ABC, 1989–92

Q34. Hannah Miller and Marty Gold were lovers who also worked as writers for *Chicago Weekly* magazine. Hannah, a beautiful woman who struggled to maintain her figure, was most proud of her breasts and had a specific name for them. What did she call them?

Q35. Hannah and her best friend, Robin, had known each other since they were five. They also lived in the same apartment building and had a nickname for each other. What was it?

Q36. In the eleventh grade, Hannah and Robin began to think about their futures and made a pact. What was it?

Q37. When Hannah and Marty dined out, they ate at what specific restaurant?

A30. Apple and Butterscotch Pecan Pie

A31. Gulliver the dog; Oscar the lizard

Angie

A32. The Liberty Coffee Shop

A33. Rose's House of Beauty

Anything but Love

A34. "The Girls"

A35. Mrs. Schmenkman

A36. If neither was married by age thirty, each would tell people her husband was with the Witness Protection Program.

A37. Marino's

Anything but Love continued

Q38. Marty enjoyed being with Hannah, but there were times he relished going out with the boys for the kind of entertainment he felt Hannah wouldn't like. What bar did Marty frequent on these occasions?

Baby Talk
ABC, 1991–92

Q39. Maggie Campbell was a single mother struggling to raise her infant son Mickey. Mickey had type AB blood, a rubber ducky named Ralphie, and red Jell-O was his favorite food. What was his favorite song?

Q40. Thinking Mickey had acting talent, Maggie let him audition for the tropical line of baby food for what company?

Q41. When Mary Page Keller replaced Julia Duffy in the role of Maggie, she acquired a job as an accountant at what company?

Q42. James Halbrook was Maggie's romantic interest and the building's super. He is a budding songwriter and composed what TV commercial jingle?

Bachelor Father
CBS/NBC/ABC, 1957–62

Q43. A bachelor's effort to raise his pretty niece after the death of her parents was the focal point of this sitcom. Bentley Gregg was the "Bachelor Father" of the title, a private-practice attorney whose office was located in what Los Angeles building?

Q44. Kelly Gregg was the thirteen-year-old who suddenly became Bentley's responsibility. What school did she attend?

Q45. Kelly's favorite subject in school was math. She and her friends frequented what after-school hangout?

A38. Dick and Dee's International House of Mud

Baby Talk

A39. "Muskrat Love"

A40. Beacon Baby Foods

A41. Coleman Accounting

A42. Peachy Time Gum

Bachelor Father

A43. The Crescent Building

A44. Beverly Hills High

A45. Bill's Malt Shop

Benson
ABC, 1979–86

Q46. Benson DuBois was the butler to Gene Gatling, the governor of mythical Capitol City. In what community did Gene reside (the locale of the governor's mansion)?

Q47. Before entering politics, Gene was a paper mill industrialist. What was he famous for at the mill?

Q48. What was the motto of Gov. Gene Gatling's state?

Q49. Gene's personal secretary, Denise, and his press secretary, Peter, married on September 16, 1983. What was Denise's term of endearment for Peter?

Bewitched
ABC, 1964–72

Q50. Samantha and Darrin Stephens lived in Connecticut at 1164 Morning Glory Circle. On what days were the trash pickups?

Q51. When Samantha, a comely witch, had a craving for food, what was the only meal that would satisfy her?

Q52. Sam's beautiful cousin, Serena, called herself "The Goddess of Love." Of what club was Serena a member (she was also the entertainment chairperson)?

Q53. Larry Tate was Darrin's gray-haired boss at the McMahon and Tate Ad Agency. What did Serena call Larry?

Q54. Samantha's Aunt Clara was somewhat addled and was famous for her prized collection of what?

Benson

A46. Lawrence County

A47. His bunkhouse biscuits

A48. "If it's not broken, don't fix it."

A49. "Bunny Wabbitt Face"

Bewitched

A50. Tuesday and Friday

A51. Ringtail pheasant

A52. The Cosmos Club

A53. "Peter Cotton Top"

A54. Doorknobs

Blossom
NBC, 1991–95

Q55. Blossom Russo is the perfect combination "of a little sugar and a lot of spice." Although she is only thirteen, her brother Joey calls her a borderline babe—"You're in the honor society, you play the trumpet, but you haven't been visited by the hooter fairy yet." Still a kid, she sleeps with what famous TV-character doll by her side?

Q56. Blossom and her friend, Six, attend Tyler High School and love to dance. Although Blossom dances for obvious reasons, it is not the same case for Six. Why does she dance?

Q57. Anthony, Blossom's older brother, had a drug problem for four years but is now recovering. He first worked for Fatty's Pizza Parlor, then as an emergency medical technician. Who was the first celebrity he assisted?

Q58. Blossom's younger brother, Joey, believes the sun is the other side of the moon and, according to her, "if the dorks had a navy he'd be their admiral." Blossom feels that Joey has only one talent. What is it?

Q59. The family has a cat that though rarely seen is often mentioned. What is its name?

Q60. When a producer came up with an idea for a series about the Russos, what was the show originally called and what was it finally changed to?

Bob
CBS, 1992–93

Q61. Mad Dog, "Mankind's Best Friend," was the comic book creation of Bob McKay, a cartoonist for Ace Comics. What company owned Ace Comics?

Q62. Bob created Mad Dog in 1964 (he drew the concept on a napkin) and sold the idea to a publisher. It never caught on and was yanked after the twelfth issue. How many copies of the first issue were sold?

Blossom

A55.   ALF

A56.   "To get all sweaty and dizzy and see stars."

A57.   Justine Bateman, when she fell and injured her elbow

A58.   Drinking Pepsi through his nose

A59.   Scruffy

A60.   First "The Russos," then "Everything's Coming Up Rosie"

Bob

A61.   American-Canadian Transcontinental Communications

A62.   Nine

Bob *continued*

Q63. Mad Dog wore blue tights with an orange M on his chest. He also had two human assistants. Who were they?

Q64. Before her job as Bob's colorist, Trisha, his daughter, worked as a "wench waitress" at what pub?

Q65. The owner and publisher of Ace Comics was never seen, but his voice was heard over the speaker phone and his staff lived in fear of him. Who belonged to this "voice of terror"?

The Bob Newhart Show
CBS, 1972–78

Q66. Bob Hartley was a psychologist who lived with his wife, Emily, a grammar school vice principal, in Apartment 523 of a building owned by what company?

Q67. When in need of extra money, Bob took a job as an insurance salesman for a company whose motto was "We gotta insure these guys." Name the company?

Q68. Emily first taught third grade at Gorman Elementary School, then became the vice principal where?

Q69. Howard Borden, Bob's neighbor, was originally a 747 navigator. When he was replaced by a computer he found work with what airline?

Q70. Bob's secretary, Carol, lived in Apartment 7 of an unnamed building. When the doorbell rang, a tape recording of a barking dog was activated. What had Carol named the dog?

Bosom Buddies
ABC, 1980–82

Q71. Kip and Henry worked at an ad agency in Manhattan, but lived in a women-only hotel named the Susan B. Anthony. What was the name of the agency where they toiled?

A63.   Penny and Buddy

A64.   The Keg and Cleaver

A65.   Mr. TerHorst

The Bob Newhart Show

A66.   Skyline Management Corporation

A67.   Loggers Casualty Insurance

A68.   Tracy Grammar School

A69.   EDS (European Delivery Service)

A70.   Lobo

Bosom Buddies

A71.   Livingston, Gentry, and Mishkin

Bosom Buddies continued

Q72. In order to reside at the Susan B. Anthony, Henry and Kip had to dress as women. The clothes they used for this masquerade were from what clients of the agency's?

Q73. When Kip and Henry, and their coworker, Amy Cassidy, quit their jobs, they opened their own ad agency when they purchased a bankrupt commercial production studio. What did they name their company?

Q74. Kip and Henry were longtime friends who had lived in Shaker Heights near Cleveland. What school did they attend?

The Brady Bunch
ABC, 1969–74

Q75. After marrying and forming the Brady Bunch, Mike and Carol set up housekeeping on Clinton Avenue in Los Angeles. Mike designed the house. How many bedrooms and bathrooms did it have?

Q76. In the opening theme, the Bradys (and Alice the housekeeper) were seen in a tic-tac-toe board. Jan, Alice, and Peter were in the middle squares from left to right. Who occupied the top and bottom squares, left to right?

Q77. Marcia and Jan Brady both attended Westdale High School and worked after school at what ice cream parlor?

Q78. When Jan, the middle girl, felt she was not as pretty as Marcia, she pretended to have a boyfriend. What did she call him?

Q79. Cindy, the youngest of the girls, had a Kitty Carry-All doll and two pet rabbits. What did she call the rabbits?

Q80. Greg, the oldest of the boys, formed a singing group called the Brady Six with his brothers and sisters and tried to break into the music business on his own. What name did he use?

A72.   Blouse City and Dresses for Women

A73.   60 Seconds Street

A74.   Edgar Allen Poe High

The Brady Bunch

A75.   Four bedrooms, two bathrooms

A76.   Top: Marcia, Carol, Greg; bottom: Cindy, Mike, Bobby

A77.   Hanson's

A78.   George Glass

A79.   Romeo and Juliet

A80.   Johnny Bravo

The Brady Bunch continued

Q81. Joan of Arc was Cindy's hero; Jesse James was Bobby's. What real person did middle boy Peter mention as being his hero?

Q82. It turned his sisters' hair orange, but Bobby, the youngest Brady thought he could make a million dollars by selling what product?

Bridget Loves Bernie
CBS, 1972–73

Q83. Bridget Fitzgerald was Catholic; Bernie Steinberg was Jewish. They met, fell in love, married, and set up housekeeping in an apartment over Steinberg's Delicatessen on Manhattan's Lower East Side. Bernie drove a taxi, and at what school did Bridget teach?

Q84. Bernie's parents, Sam and Sophie, owned the deli over which Bridget and Bernie lived. Bridget's rich parents were Walter and Amy. What company did Walter own?

Q85. IC-56 was the license plate of the cab driven by Bernie. What was his cab number?

Captain Nice
NBC, 1967

Q86. When he tried to join the army, they burned his draft card. When he enrolled in a self-defense course, "They said I should carry an axe." He was afraid of girls, was ordinary and didn't stand out. He was Carter Nash, a nebbishy police chemist who invented a liquid that transformed him into Captain Nice, a daring crime fighter. Where did Carter get the inspiration to name his alter ego?

Q87. After drinking his invention, something happened before lightning struck and transformed Carter into Captain Nice. What was it?

A81. George Washington

A82. Neat and Natural Hair Tonic

Bridget Loves Bernie

A83. Immaculate Heart Academy

A84. Global Investments

A85. Cab number 12

Captain Nice

A86. From the initials on his belt buckle—C.N.

A87. Carter hiccupped

Captain Nice continued

Q88. Carter's mother knew that her son was the heroic Captain Nice, but his father was not aware of Carter's alias and not even particularly aware of Carter. When Mr. Nash couldn't remember Carter's name, what did he call him?

Car 54, Where Are You?
NBC, 1961–63

Q89. Gunther Toody and Francis Muldoon were police officers with the 53rd Precinct in the Bronx. They rode together in patrol car 54 and were members of what fraternity?

Q90. Francis was single while Gunther was married to the always nagging Lucille. What was Lucille's maiden name?

Q91. Francis lived with his mother and sister, Peggy. Mrs. Muldoon had a fascination with what movie idol after whom she named her son?

Q92. The henpecked Leo Schnauser was also an officer with the 53rd. Sylvia, his wife, was always suspicious when he went out for a night with Toody and Muldoon. What did Sylvia think Leo was doing on these occasions?

Charles in Charge
Syndicated, 1987–90

Q93. Charles was the live-in housekeeper to the Powell family in New Jersey while he attended college. What was its name?

Q94. While Charles was majoring in education, his friend, Buddy, had been told that aptitude tests indicated that he was best qualified for jury duty. What was Buddy's real first name?

A88. Spot

Car 54, Where Are You?

A89. The Brotherhood Club

A90. Hasselwhite

A91. Francis X. Bushman

A92. Having a secret affair with Marilyn Monroe

Charles in Charge

A93. Copeland College

A94. Buddence

Charles in Charge continued

Q95. Buddy lived in the college dorm with his pet lizard Lloyd, and ant, Arlo. As a kid, Buddy had not only a hand puppet he called Handie but a dog, also. What did he call the pooch?

Q96. Jamie, the oldest of the Powell children, was an exceptionally pretty teenager. Her good looks got her a role in what TV commercial?

Q97. While Jamie was growing into a beautiful woman, her father still saw her as a little girl. What did he call her?

Q98. Sarah, the middle child, was sensitive and longed to be a writer. Ross was the name of her pet turtle. What was her favorite doll's name?

Q99. The mythical college Charles attended had a mascot. What was it?

The Charmings
ABC, 1987–88

Q100. When told by her magic mirror that she was not the fairest of all, the evil queen, Lillian, cast a spell on Snow White. The spell backfired and suspended Lillian, Snow White, Snow's husband, Eric Charming, and their children, Thomas and Cory, a thousand years. They awoke to a new life in 1987, and Snow White now worked as a fashion designer, with Eric a children's story book author. What was the name of the first book he wrote?

Q101. Lillian—maiden name was Lipschitz—suffered from P.M.S. (Post Magic Syndrome) once every twenty-eight years, and had a pet thing (an unknown creature) and a crow. Name either the thing or the crow.

Q102. Other pets in the Charming household were Eric's horse and Thomas and Cory's lizard. Give the name for either one.

A95.   Kitty

A96.   Banana Cream Shampoo and Hair Lotion

A97.   "Little Scooter"

A98.   Rebecca

A99.   Mr. Hobbs, the goat

The Charmings

A100.   *The Four Billy Goats Gruff*

A101.   Muffin was the thing; Quoth was the crow.

A102.   The horse was Gendel; the lizard was Spike.

Cheers
NBC, 1982–93

Q103. The bar at 112½ Beacon Street in Boston was Cheers, "the place where everybody knows your name." What was the legal capacity according to a notice that was posted above the door?

Q104. When Sam Malone, the current bar owner, was a ballplayer, he found something that he used as a good luck charm. What was it?

Q105. Diane Chambers was the first barmaid. In addition to being an art student and substitute teacher at Boston University, she held two other jobs. Name one of them.

Q106. Rebecca Howe was part of the large corporation that purchased Cheers after Sam originally sold it. What was her computer password for the corporation?

Q107. Rebecca often wondered why she took the job as the bar's business manager as it caused her nothing but aggravation. Watching what favorite TV show usually calmed her?

Q108. Ernie Pantusso, called Coach, was Sam's original bartender. He also had another nickname as pitching coach for the Boston Red Sox. What was it?

Q109. Carla was Sam's nasty, wisecracking, oft-married waitress. She attended St. Clete's School for Wayward Girls, and this is probably the most difficult question in the book: What was Carla's full name?

Q110. At what bar did Carla work before Sam hired her?

Q111. When she was a kid, Diane's father called her "Muffin" because she was sweet; as a kid Carla was also called "Muffin" by her brothers. Why?

Q112. Bar regular Cliff Claven was a mailman assigned to the South Central Branch. Besides the dog on his route, Cliff feared one thing because it put an extra strain on him. What was it?

Cheers

A103. 75 people

A104. A bottle cap

A105. Salesgirl at the Third Eye Bookstore or checker at Hurley's Market

A106. Sweet Baby

A107. *Spenser: For Hire*

A108. "Red" (not because he had red hair but because he once read a book)

A109. Carla Maria Victoria Angelina Teresa Appollonia Lozupone Tortelli LeBec

A110. The Broken Spoke

A111. Because her brothers stuffed her ears with yeast and tried to bake her face.

A112. The day the Sears catalogue came out

Cheers continued

Q113. Norm Peterson was another regular who loved to eat, drink, and run up large bar tabs. Married to the unseen Vera, he was a CPA. What was Norm's real first name?

Q114. Woody Boyd became Sam's bartender after Coach's death. He was born in Hanover, Indiana, and was known for inventing what game?

Q115. Bar regular Frasier Crane is a psychiatrist who considered himself "the solver of all things personal," and conducted self-help seminars that cost $350. What did he call them?

Q116. "Frost Warning" was the term Cliff uses when Frasier's wife, Lilith, entered the bar. Lilith was also a psychiatrist who "rides the roost in her bra and panties," according to Frasier. What book had Lilith written that made her famous?

Clarissa Explains It All
Nickelodeon, 1991–95

Q117. Clarissa Darling is a thirteen-year-old who doesn't particularly like her name. "Anything without a last name would have been great" she says, "but no one asked me." Clarissa lives at 464 Shadow Lane in what town?

Q118. Many people have a dog for protection, but not our Clarissa. She has a pet alligator she calls Elvis, who lives in a small plastic pool in Clarissa's room. What has she named the pool?

Q119. Clarissa's mother, Janet, is a vitamin freak and health food nut whose Zucchini lentil surprise is her favorite dinner. What is her favorite dessert?

Q120. Marshall, Clarissa's father, is an architect. By what term of endearment does he call Clarissa?

A113. Hilary

A114. Hide Bob's Pants

A115. "The Crane Train to Mental Well Being"

A116. *Good Girls/Bad Boys*

Clarissa Explains It All

A117. Baxter Beach

A118. The Heartbreak Hotel

A119. Carob pudding cake with whipped tofu topping

A120. "Sport"

The Cosby Show
NBC, 1984–92

Q121. The Huxtable Family lived at 10 Stigwood Avenue in Brooklyn. Cliff, the father, was an obstetrician who worked from his home and at two hospitals. One was Corinthian Hospital. What was the other?

Q122. Both Cliff and his wife, Clair, attended Hillman College in Georgia. Clair majored in law and worked for what firm?

Q123. Attending Hillman College was a Huxtable tradition, but Sondra, the oldest child, was the first to break it. It cost Cliff and Clair $79,648.72 to send their daughter to what college?

Q124. Denise, the second born, was the most troublesome of the Huxtable kids. She quit Hillman after three semesters and had a couple of jobs before marrying Martin Kendall. Name one of the two jobs Denise held.

Q125. Cliff and Clair's only son, Theo, was the second to break tradition when he attended NYU. In high school Theo was a member of the wrestling team. What did they call him?

Q126. Vanessa, the fourth child, also broke tradition (she attended the University of Philadelphia). What was the name of the rock group Vanessa joined while in high school?

Q127. Impish Rudy was the youngest Huxtable. Vanilla was her favorite flavor of ice cream and she played on a Pee Wee League football team. She had a teddy bear and a goldfish. Rudy called the goldfish Lamont, but what was the name of her teddy bear?

Q128. Sondra married Elvin, a medical student who eventually became a doctor, although he almost gave it up for a psychological reason. What was it?

The Cosby Show

A121. Children's Hospital

A122. Greentree, Bradley, and Dexter

A123. Princeton

A124. Salesgirl at the Wilderness Store; assistant to the executive assistant at Blue Wave Records

A125. "Monster Man Huxtable"

A126. The Lipsticks

A127. Bobo

A128. He had a problem charging people for medical help.

Davis Rules
CBS, 1991–92

Q129. Dwight Davis, a widower, lived in Seattle with his children, Robbie, Charlie, and Ben, and his father, Gunny, at 631 Evergreen. He taught math, science, and history and was also the principal of what grammar school?

Q130. Dwight loved golf, but played only three times a year. He hung out at what golfing store where he was called a "browse-aholic"?

Q131. Gunny, whose real name was William Davis, got the nickname during his service with the marines. What did he call the USMC?

Q132. Gunny now cared for the family. A great cook, he could make top-notch stew out of what?

Q133. Gwen, Dwight's effervescent sister, came to live with the family in second-season episodes. For what radio station did Gwen work?

Dear John
NBC, 1988–92

Q134. John Lacey one day returned home from work to find a Dear John letter from his wife, Wendy. How long were they married before she left him?

Q135. In an attempt to adjust to the single life, John joined the One-on-One Club. On what night did the club hold its meetings?

Q136. Now living in Apartment 42 on Woodhaven Boulevard in Manhattan, John cared for the three cats of his unseen ninety-two-year-old neighbor. Name the pets.

Q137. Pretty club member Mary Beth Sutton had been a homecoming queen and always expected the best to happen. For what airline magazine did she work?

Davis Rules

A129. Pomahac Elementary School

A130. Par for the Course

A131. "Uncle Sam's Miserable Children"

A132. Roadkill

A133. KPLG

Dear John

A134. Ten years

A135. Fridays

A136. Snuffy, Fluffy, and Snowball

A137. *Above the Clouds*

Dear John continued

Q138. Ralph Drang, the always-worried Lincoln Tunnel toll-booth attendant, lived by himself and had decorated his bedroom with wallpaper from what famous TV show?

Q139. Overconfident schemer and con artist Kirk Morris lost his wife to another woman. What was the name of the catering company that he and his friend, Denise, operated?

December Bride
CBS, 1954–59

Q140. Lily Ruskin, a young-at-heart sixty-year-old widow, lived with her married daughter, Ruth Henshaw, and son-in-law Matt at 728 Elm Street in Westwood, California. What was unique about the block on which they resided?

Q141. Lily sought to help people either in person or through the newspaper column she wrote for the *Los Angeles Gazette*. What was her column called?

Q142. Next-door neighbor Peter Porter claimed that "I'm not henpecked, I'm buzzardpecked." He was, of course, referring to his never-seen wife, Gladys. What did Pete say were the symbols of his marriage?

Q143. When the show *Pete and Gladys* was spun off into a series of its own, one of the characters Pete mentioned on *December Bride*—their daughter—was not used. What was her name?

Delta
ABC, 1992–93

Q144. Patsy Cline was the idol of Delta Bishop, a Mississippi hairdresser who dreamt of becoming a country singer. Where did Delta work before moving to Nashville to pursue her dream?

A138. *Star Trek*

A139. Cuisine by Kirk

December Bride

A140. As Matt said: "It is lined with Palm Trees. One block over is Palm Street which is lined with Elm Trees."

A141. "Tips for Housewives"

A142. "A padlock, chains, and a straightjacket."

A143. Linda

Delta

A144. Mona's House of Hair

Delta *continued*

Q145. In Nashville, Delta acquired a job at the Green Lantern, a bar where Patsy Cline supposedly sang. It was owned by Darden Towe, a former stockbroker who bought it as a way of escaping his hectic life. After his marriage broke up, he became its full-time operator and wrote "an awful gladiator novel." What was the name of the work?

Q146. Delta resided in an apartment over the garage of a house owned by her cousin, Lavonne. At what beauty salon did Lavonne work?

Designing Women
CBS, 1986–93

Q147. Sisters Julia and Suzanne Sugarbaker owned a chic interior decorating firm in Atlanta. From what store do they buy their goods?

Q148. Julia was the more sophisticated sister. "To get a vacation from being myself" (to find her spiritual self), Julia changed her name to Giselle and sang at what nightclub?

Q149. Totally self-absorbed Suzanne flaunted her sexuality to get what she wanted. Although objecting to this, Julia was very proud of Suzanne for winning what beauty title?

Q150. Charlene Frazier was the office manager at Sugarbakers, but took a second job to help pay the bills. What was her other job?

Q151. Mary Jo Shively, the divorced mother of two, was the firm's buyer. Although her dog was never seen, she talked about him frequently. What was his name?

Q152. Allison Sugarbaker, Julia's cousin, came on the scene in 1991 when Suzanne took off for Japan. Allison sobbed at everything and suffered from what she called O.P.D. What was this?

A145. *I, Dardenius*

A146. Thelma's Hairdressers

Designing Women

A147. Fabric World

A148. The Blue Note Cafe

A149. Miss Georgia World of 1976

A150. Salesgirl for Kemper Cosmetics

A151. Brownie

A152. Obnoxious Personality Disorder

Designing Women continued

Q153. When Charlene moved to England, her down-home sister, Carlene, joined the firm. Where did Carlene work before Sugarbakers?

Q154. Anthony Bouvier is the ex-con who became the firm's delivery man. Where did he serve time for his part in a liquor store robbery?

Q155. During the series' final season, Anthony married a beautiful showgirl named Etienne Toussant, who worked at the Tropicana Resort and Casino and referred to Anthony as "Tony, 'cause he's my tiger." What did Etienne like to be called?

The Dick Van Dyke Show
CBS, 1961–66

Q156. Rob Petrie met Laura Meeker while stationed at the Camp Crowder Army Base in Joplin, Missouri. He was a sergeant; she was a USO girl. While doing a song and dance number together, Rob, who was wearing combat boots, stepped on Laura's foot and broke her toes. Name the song to which they were performing.

Q157. Rob and Laura married while he was still in the service and set up housekeeping first on the army base, then in Ohio when Rob was discharged. He found work as a disc jockey at what radio station?

Q158. After an interview with TV star Alan Brady, Rob got a job as his head writer in New York City. *The Alan Brady Show* was rated number one in Liberia; what was its ranking in the U.S.?

Q159. Several of Alan Brady's companies paid the bills. Rob got his checks from the Ishomor Company; the show's band was paid by Brady Lady (named after Alan's wife). What company, named for Alan's mother-in-law, paid Rob's fellow writers, Sally Rogers and Buddy Sorrell?

A153. Ray Flat's Flatbed Furniture Store

A154. Cell Block D of Atlanta State Prison

A155. "E.T."

The Dick Van Dyke Show

A156. "You Wonderful You"

A157. WOFF

A158. Number 17

A159. Barracuda, Ltd.

The Dick Van Dyke Show *continued*

Q160. Rob and Laura lived in New Rochelle, New York. In the basement of their house, behind some loose bricks in back of the furnace, Laura hid something from Rob. What was it?

Q161. One night, when Rob couldn't sleep, he decided to count the roses on his bedroom wallpaper. How many roses were there?

Q162. Before the birth of Rob and Laura's son, Ritchie, everybody suggested a name for him. Laura wanted Robert or Roberta; Rob, Laura or Lawrence. Sally suggested Valentino ("I was saving it for a parakeet, but you can have it"), and show producer Mel Cooley suggested three names: Allen, Allan, and Alan. What name did Buddy suggest?

Q163. At Herbie's Hiawatha Lodge, one could catch Buddy and Sally performing a comical song and dance routine. By what names did they bill themselves?

Q164. Buddy once had his own show, *Buddy's Bag*, and also worked as a writer on *The Billy Barrows Show*. What is Buddy's real first name?

Q165. Sally was single and looking for Mr. Right. She dated Herman Glimshire, a mama's boy, and had two cats. One was named Mr. Henderson; what did she call the other?

A Different World
NBC, 1987–93

Q166. Hillman College in Georgia was not just a tough school, "it was a butt breaker." Cliff and Clair Huxtable's daughter, Denise, enrolled there, but couldn't seem to achieve the *As* and *Bs* she got in high school. What was her grade average after three semesters (when she dropped out)?

Q167. While Denise didn't keep track of the checks she wrote ("I'm in college now. I'm busy, I have responsibilities"), she did bring something to cheer up the dorm room she shared with Maggie and Jaleesa. What was it?

A160. Her old love letters from high school boyfriend Joe Coogan

A161. 382½

A162. "Exit. If the kid is an actor, it'll be in every theater in the country."

A163. Gilbert and Solomon

A164. Maurice

A165. Mr. Diefenthaler

A Different World

A166. 1.7 (One point seven)

A167. A deer lamp with lights on the antlers

A Different World continued

Q168. Maggie, an army brat, left Hillman at the same time as Denise when her father was transferred overseas. While Denise had an undecided major, Maggie was determined to become something. What was her major?

Q169. Whitley Gilbert was one of the most beautiful girls at Hillman. She hailed from Richmond, Virginia, where her father was a judge, and her passion was art and shopping. Very proud of the fact that her beauty allowed her to steal men from other girls, vain Whitley would use a bar of soap only once and could not stand anyone else touching or wearing her clothes. She would not under any circumstances eat what food—or allow anyone to eat it in her presence?

Q170. He wore "those funny-looking flip-down sunglasses that drive you crazy" and he hit on almost every girl in sight. He was Dwayne Wayne, who pursued a math degree. Dwayne's middle name was Creofus; but when he had a talk show on the school radio station, what did he call himself?

Diff'rent Strokes
NBC/ABC, 1978–86

Q171. Although the daughter of a rich father (Phillip Drummond), Kimberly wanted to make money on her own. She supplemented her weekly ten-dollar allowance by taking an after-school job at what fast-food store in Manhattan?

Q172. Arnold and Willis Jackson were the two brothers Phillip adopted. Arnold, the younger, more mischievous one, had a ratty old doll named Homer, a cricket named Lucky, and a goldfish. What did he call the fish?

Q173. Arnold loved model railroading and video games. He had his railroad empire set up in his bedroom and he was the champ at what game at the Video Arcade?

Q174. While he attended a number of different grammar schools, one thing plagued Arnold no matter which one it was—the school bully. What was the bully's name?

A168. Journalism

A169 Cheese

A170. Darryl Walker

Diff'rent Strokes

A171. The Hula Hut

A172. Abraham

A173. "Space Sucker"

A174. The Gooch

Diff'rent Strokes continued

Q175. As a kid, older brother Willis had a doll named Wendy Wetems. He also had a favorite expression ("Say what?") and he formed a rock band that featured his sister and his girlfriend, Charlene, as lead singers. What was the name of the band?

Dinosaurs
ABC, 1991–93

Q176. It was the year 60,000,003 B.C. and dinosaurs had come out of the forests to marry and raise a family. Human beings of this era were portrayed as a less-intelligent life form. One dinosaur family, the Sinclairs, had a pet human (a cavegirl). What was her name?

Q177. Earl Sinclair, wife Fran, and children Charlene and Robbie lived as suburbanites in the town of Pangaea. What was the symbol of supremacy in a dinosaur house?

Q178. In the first episode, the family was blessed with another mouth to feed when Baby Sinclair was hatched. The entire household was shocked when Baby spoke his first word (a gutter word in this world). What was it?

Q179. Baby seemed to recognize everybody in the family but his father, Earl, and hit him on the head with a frying pan, saying, "Not the mama!" By what brand of pan did Earl get hit over the head?

Q180. Fran shopped for food at the Swamp Basket and prepared such dishes as waffle meat pancakes. What was the family's favorite breakfast cereal?

Q181. Earl and Fran had been married for nineteen years when the series began. Where did Earl keep the marriage license?

Q182. The Job Wizard decreed what job each dinosaur will hold and the Elders ruled the land. From where did the Elders rule?

Q183. Wars had been started over it and it was a rare treat, but it was a favorite dinosaur snack. What was it?

A175. The Afro Desiacs

Dinosaurs

A176. Sparky

A177. Possession of the TV remote control

A178. "Smoo"

A179. A Myman Frying Pan

A180. Boo Boo Bears Cereal

A181. Under the TV to balance it

A182. The Cave of Destiny

A183. Pistachio nuts

Dobie Gillis
CBS, 1959–63

Q184. Herbert T. Gillis and his wife, Winnie, owned the Gillis Grocery Store, where their girl-crazy teenage son, Dobie, worked. Known as a cheapskate, Herbert was voted "the citizen most likely to hang on to his last dollar." He frequented the Scarpitta Barber Shop and was a member of what fraternity?

Q185. Dobie was most famous for his infatuation with the beautiful but vain Thalia Menninger. Dobie was usually penniless, but Thalia has plans to improve him so he could make "oodles and oodles of money." What was Thalia's favorite perfume that, at $18 an ounce, Dobie couldn't afford to buy her?

Q186. Maynard G. Krebs, Dobie's bearded beatnik friend, loved to play the bongos and was a hip jazz fan. Where did Maynard hang out (where he played records so much that he wore out the grooves)?

Q187. Maynard had a weekly allowance of thirty-five cents and loved to watch the movie *The Monster That Devoured Cleveland*. He also liked to drive but failed his driving test how many times in how many years?

Q188. Maynard had the world's largest collection of tinfoil, three cousins named Flopsy, Mopsy, and Cottontail, and a stuffed armadillo. What was the name of his pet critter?

Q189. Chatsworth Osborne, Jr., the filthy rich, spoiled heir to the Osborne banking fortune, called his mother "Mumsey." What did she call him?

Q190. Chatsworth had type R (for Royal) blood and belonged to what club at S. Peter Pryor College?

Dobie Gillis

A184. The Benevolent Order of the Bison Lodge

A185. "MMMM"

A186. Riff Ryan's Music Store

A187. Forty-six times in six years

A188. Herman

A189. "You nasty boy"

A190. The Silver Spoons Club

The Donna Reed Show
ABC, 1958–66

Q191. Dr. Alex Stone, his wife, Donna, and their children, Mary and Jeff, lived in the small town of Hilldale in the fifth district. What distinguished this house from the others on the block?

Q192. A pediatrician, Alex was just an intern when he met and married Donna Mullinger, a nurse. During their honeymoon Alex heard one song so many times that he came to hate it. What song was it?

Q193. Daughter Mary was three years older than Jeff, hung out with her friends at Kelzey's Malt Shop, and enjoyed dancing at the Round Robin. What size dress did Mary wear?

Q194. As a kid Jeff put on puppet shows for his friends. What was the name of the puppet he used?

Q195. Jeff was a member of the Bobcats football team and his favorite TV show was *Gunbutt*. What product sponsored the show?

The Duck Factory
NBC, 1984

Q196. Buddy Winkler Productions produced a Saturday morning cartoon series called *The Dippy Duck Show*. The network that aired the series was not named and put it on for only one reason. What was it?

Q197. The daring Dippy, a duck who battled for right, had a number of enemies. Name one of them.

Q198. The beautiful Sherry Jurwalski was a topless Las Vegas ice skater who married Buddy Winkler and inherited the Winkler empire when he died three weeks later. What did Aggie, the animation director, call Sherry?

The Donna Reed Show

A191. A carob tree on the front lawn

A192. "Melancholy Baby"

A193. Eight

A194. Bongo

A195. Happy Gum—the All-Purpose Chewing Gum

The Duck Factory

A196. They got it cheap.

A197. Irving the Terrible and Rotten Renaldo

A198. The Widow Winkler

Duffy's Tavern
NBC, 1954

Q199. Duffy's Tavern was where "the elite meet to eat" and where, with a beer, the free lunch costs fifteen cents. The Feinschmecker Brewery of Greater Staten Island serviced the tavern. What beer did Duffy order?

Q200. Located on a shabby section of New York's Third Avenue, Duffy's Tavern had a caring attitude about its customers ("We don't roll customers until they're drunk," said Archie the bartender). But the tavern also lost money on rainy nights. Why?

Q201. Simple-minded Clifton Finnegan, Archie's friend, collected cigar bands as a hobby and never married because of what happened to his parents—"They became a mother and father." Archie also never married. What was his reason?

Empty Nest
NBC, 1988–95

Q202. A widower living with his daughters, Carol and Barbara, at 1755 Fairview Road in Miami Beach, Dr. Harry Weston had an office at the Community Medical Center. From what medical school did Harry graduate?

Q203. Harry bought his medical supplies from the Radacine Medical Supplies Company. What brand of bandages did he use for his patients?

Q204. Oldest daughter Carol laughs too loud, is a klutz at sewing, and has a dream of opening a self-help book shop. While she worked at a number of jobs (ten before the series began), she had two we know of—the assistant director of the University of Miami Rare Books Library and a catering business she later began. What is the name of her company?

Q205. Carol is good with money and has fat attacks each spring. She is also a member of what support group?

Duffy's Tavern

A199. The Weehawken Lager Beer Nectar

A200. "Who wants to go out and lay in the gutter?"

A201. "I wanted my wife to have everything—money, a mansion, a big car, and a yacht, but I ain't found the right dame yet."

Empty Nest

A202. Bedford Medical School

A203. Starbright Bandages

A204. Elegant Epicure

A205. Adult Children of Perfectly Fine Parents

Empty Nest continued

Q206. Sister Barbara is terrible with money and works as a police officer. Her favorite comic strip is *Beetle Bailey* and she and her father wrote a book. What did they call it?

Q207. Barbara collects backscratchers and uses what antiperspirant? (It's "the official antiperspirant of the Miss Junior Teen USA Pageant.")

Q208. As kids, Carol and Barbara attended Camp Weemawalk. Barbara was called "Swim Like a Fish." What was Carol called?

Q209. When Kristy McNichol (who played Barbara) left the series due to manic depression, Harry's previously unseen youngest daughter, Emily, was brought on. What college was Emily attending?

Q210. Laverne Todd, Harry's brash nurse-receptionist, is from Hickory, Arkansas. To get home for visits, Laverne takes a plane to Little Rock, then what private charter plane to Hickory?

Q211. To protect her job, Laverne has a secret decoder to unscramble her filing system. Her maiden name is Higbee, she reads the *National Inquisitor*, and she wears what shade of lipstick?

Q212. The obnoxious, food-pilfering Charlie Dietz is Harry's neighbor. Charlie considers himself a ladies' man and is the fifth assistant purser on what luxury liner?

Evening Shade
CBS, 1990–94

Q213. Wood Newton is the football coach of the Mules, the high school team in Evening Shade, Arkansas. He is married to Ava, the town's prosecuting attorney, and they are the parents of three children (Molly, Will, and Taylor). What was Wood's nickname when he played football at Evening Shade High?

A206. *Jumpy Goes to the Hospital*

A207. "Zesty"

A208. "Stay in Tent"

A209. The Hollyoak Girls School

A210. Dwayne's Plane

A211. Passion Pink

A212. *The Ocean Queen*

Evening Shade

A213. Thumper

Evening Shade continued

Q214. Wood next attended the University of Arkansas and became a quarterback for the Pittsburgh Steelers. He wore jersey number 22 and had what nickname?

Q215. Ava has been married to Wood for fifteen years. As a kid, she was called "Chubby" Evans, and it took her two years to lose the weight. In the house she shares with Wood, Ava has one cherished possession. What is it?

Q216. Molly is eleven years old, wears a size 5½ shoe, and attends Evening Shade Grammar School. Her favorite movie is *The Wizard of Oz* and she entered the Little Miss Evening Shade Contest (she lost when she fell attempting to wear high heels). When Molly began to fill out, she wanted a particular bra. Which one was it?

Q217. Harlan Eldridge, the town doctor, and his wife, Merleen, live on an estate they call Tara. What is the name of Harlan's boat?

Q218. Merleen believes that she exudes sexuality and is a magnet to perverts. She is most proud of three pictures that hang on the wall of her home. What are they of?

Q219. Nub Oliver delivers the town's newspaper from his little wagon. He claims to have seen every movie that was ever made and has named his paper wagon after one of them. What is it called?

F Troop
ABC, 1965–67

Q220. Fort Courage was an army fort in Kansas (1866) that had been named after the distinguished general Sam Courage. Before Capt. Wilton Parmenter became its commander, who was in charge of the fort?

Q221. Prior to his promotion as captain, Parmenter was a private with the Union Quartermaster Corps. What were his duties?

A214. Clutch

A215. Her antique bathroom window

A216. The Littlest Angel Bra

A217. Tara of the Sea

A218. Billy Graham, an American Indian, and Tom Selleck

A219. Chariot of Fire

F Troop

A220. "Cannonball" Bill McCormick

A221. Doing the officers' laundry

F Troop continued

Q222. O'Rourke Enterprises was the not-exactly-legal business venture run by crafty Sgt. Morgan O'Rourke and his vice president, Corp. Randolph Agarn. Besides the Fort Courage Saloon, what else comprises O'Rourke Enterprises?

Q223. When Agarn bought his way out of the army to manage a somewhat anachronistic rock group called the Bedbugs, O'Rourke organized his own band to discourage Agarn and get him to reenlist. What was O'Rourke's group called?

Q224. Comely Wrangler Jane owned Wrangler Jane's, the combination off-post post office and general store. In love with Wilton, she had set her sights on him and tried to wrangle a proposal. Jane could shoot, rope, and trickride a horse. What was the name of her horse?

The Facts of Life
NBC, 1979–88

Q225. Blair, Jo, Tootie, and Natalie were four teenagers who attended the Eastland School for Girls in Peekskill, New York. Blair, the most beautiful girl at the academy, was conceited, a snob, and heir to the Warner Textile Industries. She won a number of awards at Eastland. Name at least two of the three awards that were mentioned.

Q226. Blair's complete opposite was Jo, a poor Bronx girl with a tough exterior, who was at Eastland on a scholarship and was always in need of extra money. What was the name of the business she and fellow students Tootie and Natalie tried to launch?

Q227. Tootie, the youngest of the girls, wanted to become an actress. In what show did she have the lead that made her the first black girl in the school's history to play the role?

Q228. Natalie had ambitions to become a journalist and worked as a reporter for the *Peekskill Press*. What was the title of her first article while at Eastland?

A222. The International Trading Company

A223. The Termites

A224. Pecos

The Facts of Life

A225. Eastland Harvest Queen; Most Naturally Blonde; and Small Business Woman's Association Award (for inventing contour top sheets)

A226. Mama Rosa's Original Bronx Pizza, Inc.

A227. Juliet in *Romeo and Juliet*

A228. "An Eighth Grader Gets Angry"

The Facts of Life continued

Q229. When Mrs. Garrett, the school dietitian, couldn't get a raise and the school lost her pension fund, she quit to open Edna's Edibles, a gourmet food store. What was the name of the place Edna took over?

Family Matters
ABC, 1989–

Q230. Carl and Harriette Winslow reside at 263 Pinehurst Street in Chicago with their children, Edward, Laura, and Judy. Carl was first an officer, then a sergeant with what division of the police department?

Q231. In his youth, Carl was an expert pool player. At the Corner Pocket, where he played pool, he had a nickname. What was it?

Q232. Carl also held a job as a TV traffic reporter on the four o'clock news of what TV station?

Q233. Harriette is the security director at the *Chicago Chronicle*. What job at the paper did she hold prior to acquiring this one?

Q234. Middle child Laura is pretty, fashion conscious, and bright. What is the scent of her favorite perfume?

Q235. Rachel is Harriette's beautiful younger sister and she also lives with the family. When Laura's favorite after-school hangout burned down, Rachel reopened it as a diner called Rachel's Place. What was the original name?

Q236. Steve Urkel met Laura Winslow in kindergarten. She made him eat Playdoh and he has been in love with her ever since. A straight A student, Steve has a stay-away fund (his relatives send him money so he will not visit them), and Laura too, wants nothing to do with him. In a home economics class the unthinkable happened: he got a C and fainted. What caused Steve to get a C?

A229.   Ara's Deli

Family Matters

A230.   Metro Division of the Eighth Precinct

A231.   "Rack and Roll Winslow"

A232.   WNTW, Channel 13

A233.   Elevator operator

A234.   "Rainbow Cloud"

A235.   LeRoy's

A236.   He tried to make bread but the yeast didn't rise.

Family Matters continued

Q237. The equipment manager of the golf club at school, Steve boasts about being 98 percent brain and 2 percent brawn. He also has a very unusual favorite snack. What is it?

Family Ties
NBC, 1982–89

Q238. Steven Keaton and Elyse O'Donnell, flower children who met in college in the late 1960s, married after attending Woodstock and set up housekeeping in a commune where their first son, Alex, was born. Alex was the second-choice name; what was the first?

Q239. In college, Steven was president of the south campus aluminum can recycling program. He also wrote a play. What was it called?

Q240. Elyse had always dreamed of becoming a folksinger, but turned her talents to becoming an architect. What was the first structure Elyse designed?

Q241. Studious Alex P. Keaton, who had a collection of his report cards from nursery school through college, worshipped money and prided himself on being different. At Leland College, Alex had a radio program that mixed blues music with business news. What was the program called?

Q242. Alex majored in economics and accepted a job with what Wall Street firm?

Q243. Mallory, the second-born child, was very pretty and bright in her own way, with dreams of becoming a fashion designer. She had what she called a special gift for this profession. What is it?

Q244. A devout mall-shopper, Mallory attended Grant College, which "is conveniently located near all major highways." She also wrote a column for the *Columbus Shoppers' Guide*. What was it called?

A237. Anchovy paste on a dog biscuit

Family Ties

A238. Moon Muffin

A239. *A Draft Card for Burning*

A240. The Cavanaugh Building in Columbus

A241. "Syncopated Money"

A242. O'Brien, Mathers, and Clark

A243. Being able to tell fabrics apart blindfolded

A244. "Dear Mallory"

Family Ties continued

Q245. While her family disapproved of him, Mallory was crazy in love with grungy-looking Nick Moore, a struggling artist. What was the first painting Nick sold?

Q246. Jennifer was the third child, a member of the Sunshine Girls Club who attended Harding High School. She also had an after-school job at what fast-food store?

Father Knows Best
CBS/NBC/ABC, 1954–62

Q247. Jim and Margaret Anderson lived in the small town of Springfield with their children Betty, Bud, and Kathy. Jim was the all-around problem solver although he claimed "I'm just an ordinary guy who sells insurance." For whom did Jim work?

Q248. Jim and Margaret donated $25 each year to the Children's Home Society, and Margaret was a member of the Women's Club of Springfield. What daily paper did they read?

Q249. Betty was the oldest of the children and the smartest as well as the most sensitive. When something troubled Betty, she retreated to the edge of a brook in Sycamore Grove Park to sort things out. What did she call this spot?

Flying Blind
Fox, 1992–93

Q250. Alicia and Neal were lovers, two opposites who found an attraction to each other. At what restaurant in New York City did they meet?

Q251. The sexy Alicia, who worked as a model, once was an actress and became famous for what horror film produced by Specter Films?

A245. "Woman With a Half-Eaten Hamburger"

A246. Chicken Heaven

Father Knows Best

A247. The General Insurance Company

A248. The *Springfield Star News*

A249. Her Secret Thinking Place

Flying Blind

A250. The Apollo

A251. *Bride of the Marsh Monster*

Flying Blind continued

Q252. *Beverly Hills, 9021-Dead* and *Massacre at Cleavage Farm* were two other films produced by Specter, the low-budget movie company that employed Neal. Name at least one other film that was mentioned which the company produced.

The Fresh Prince of Bel Air
NBC, 1990–

Q253. Will Smith is the "Fresh Prince" of the title, a troubled West Philly teenager who is sent to live with rich relatives, Philip and Vivian Banks in Bel Air in an attempt to straighten him out. Now enrolled in the prestigious Bel Air Academy, Will earns extra spending money by working as a waiter in what restaurant?

Q254. As a kid Philip lived on a farm in Nebraska and won the Young Farmers of America Pig Passing Contest four years in a row. What was the name of his pet pig?

Q255. Vivian is a professor who substitutes at various schools. She loves gourmet meals and is nuts about one particular flavor of ice cream. What is it?

Q256. Twenty-one-year-old Hilary is Philip and Vivian's oldest child. She is beautiful and very feminine and has her hair done at what parlor?

Q257. When Hilary was nine, she took up the violin but gave it up "because it irritated my chin." She next took up ballet, but soon gave that up. Why?

Q258. Carlton, the middle child, hopes to follow in his father's footsteps and become a lawyer. He is a member of the school's poetry and glee clubs and had his first crush on what TV character?

A252. *The Revenge of the Mutant Ozone Mermaids* and *Frosty the Maniac*

The Fresh Prince of Bel Air

A253. The Brawny Deep

A254. Melvin

A255. Vanilla Swiss Almond

A256. Black Beauty

A257. "Because I thought I would get feet like Fred Flintstone."

A258. Tootie (from *The Facts of Life*)

Full House
ABC, 1987–95

Q259. Friday is "Mop the floors till you drop day" at the Tanner house in San Francisco. Danny Tanner, a widower with three daughters (D.J., Stephanie, and Michelle), now cohosts *Wake Up, San Francisco* with Rebecca Donaldson on Channel 8. What TV job did Danny work at before this show?

Q260. Danny is a neat freak who attributes his excessive neatness to his fifth birthday, when his mother gave him a set of vacuum cleaner attachments and called him her "special helper." At this same time Danny also had a "friend" he made from a washcloth. What did he name it?

Q261. D.J. is the oldest of the Tanner girls. She loves to shop at the mall "and spend hours in the bathroom." As a kid she had a favorite pillow. What did she call it?

Q262. D.J. wears "Passion Plum" eye shadow and held a job as "The Happy Helper" for what mall photographer?

Q263. Middle child Stephanie, whose catchphrase is "How rude," carries a Jetsons lunch box to school and has a favorite plush bear. What does she call the bear?

Q264. Danny, the coach of Stephanie's Little League Team, the Giants, is proud of his daughter for the curve ball she can throw. What does he call it?

Q265. Michelle is the baby of the family. "You got it, dude!" is her favorite expression; *The Little Mermaid* is her favorite movie, and she enjoys eating what cereal for breakfast?

Q266. Danny's brother-in-law, Jesse, and his best friend, Joey, help Danny in raising the girls. Jesse and Joey are business partners and run what commercial jingle-writing company?

Q267. Jesse, who idolizes Elvis Presley, has a band, Jesse and the Rippers. In high school Jesse was also part of another group. What was its name?

Full House

A259.   Sportscaster on *Newsbeat*

A260.   Terry the talking washcloth

A261.   Pillow Person

A262.   Tot Shots

A263.   Mr. Bear

A264.   The Tanner Twister

A265.   Honey Coated Fiber Bears

A266.   J.J. Creative Services (later, Double J Creative Services)

A267.   Discipline Problem

Full House continued

Q268. Joey is also a talented stand-up comic who got a big break when he was signed to do a TV pilot with Annette Funicello and Frankie Avalon. What was the title of the pilot?

Q269. Pretty Kimmy Gibler is D.J.'s best friend. "People say I look like Julia Roberts. I wish I was Madonna. She's rich." Kimmy cuts home economics classes ("'cause I'm gonna marry a doctor and hire a maid") and writes what column for the school newspaper?

The George Burns and Gracie Allen Show
CBS, 1950–58

Q270. "If it weren't for Gracie's antics," George Burns said, "I'd be selling ties." George and Gracie met in vaudeville, and when they first dated, he gave her flowers. Gracie saved those flowers by pressing them between the pages of what book?

Q271. "My Life With George Burns" was an article Gracie wrote for a magazine in 1952. She had to type it twice (she tried using carbon paper "but it's black and you can't see what you type on it"). In what magazine did the article appear?

Q272. George and Gracie's neighbors were Harry and Blanche Morton. Harry, a C.P.A., was very fussy and would drink only one kind of alcoholic beverage. What was it?

The Ghost and Mrs. Muir
NBC/ABC, 1968–70

Q273. Gull Cottage, in the New England town of Schooner Bay, was haunted by the ghost of a sea captain named Daniel Gregg, and went unoccupied for many years before Carolyn Muir and her children, Candy and Jonathan, moved in—despite its "curse." Though balking at having the Muirs live in his house, the Captain tolerated them. When Captain Gregg originally built the house in the 1800s, what plans did he have for it?

A268. *Surf's Up*

A269. "Madame Kimmy's Horoscope."

The George Burns and Gracie Allen Show

A270. *A Report on the Sheep Herding Industry*

A271. *Look*

A272. Blackberry cordial

The Ghost and Mrs. Muir

A273. A home for retired sailors

The Ghost and Mrs. Muir *continued*

Q274. Now that Carolyn had made the captain's cabin (Daniel's bedroom) hers, he only had one place of refuge left in the house. What room was it (Daniel called it "the wheel house")?

Q275. "Blast" and "Blasted" were the captain's favorite expressions. He has also made one part of the house his bridge (where he stood watch each night). Where was the captain's bridge?

Q276. Martha, the Muirs' housekeeper, disliked Captain Gregg even though she was unaware of his ghostly presence. What "term of endearment" did Martha use for the captain?

Gidget
ABC, 1965–66

Q277. Frances Lawrence, nicknamed "Gidget"—a girl who is not tall or a midget: a Gidget—lived in Santa Monica with her widowed father, Russ, an English professor. Her passion was surfing and she was in love with a surfer named Moondoggie. When Gidget was on the phone with her friends, and her sister (Anne) or father walked into the room, she had slang terms to warn the person she was talking to. Name either term.

Q278. When the rock band fad hit Santa Monica, Gidget formed a group, The Young People. When she found them too clean-cut, she radically changed their appearance and renamed them. What did she call them?

A274. The attic

A275. On the porch above Carolyn's room

A276. "The Old Barnacle"

Gidget

A277. "Parentville" and "Sisterville"

A278. Gidget and the Gorries

Gilligan's Island
CBS, 1964–67

Q279. The uncharted island about three hundred miles south-east of Hawaii was home to seven castaways when their ship was destroyed in a surprise storm. Among them was millionaire Thurston Howell III, called "The Wolf of Wall Street" and head of Howell Industries, who tried to make the best of a primitive lifestyle and still enjoy some past pleasures like playing polo. What was the name of the practice polo pony the Professor made for him out of bamboo?

Q280. Thurston attended SMU (Super Millionaires University) and was very insistent about the temperature of his bath water. What did it have to be?

Q281. Ginger was a gorgeous movie star who broke into show business in a mind-reading act with Merlin the Mind Reader. She later won a beauty contest. What was she voted?

Q282. *Sing a Song of Sing Sing, San Quentin Blues,* and *Mohawk Over the Moon* were three of the five movies Ginger made. Name one of the other two.

Q283. The Professor was a high school science teacher whose knowledge made life as comfortable as possible on the island. After his first week there, he made what he considered a fantastic discovery. What was it?

Good Times
CBS, 1974–79

Q284. The Evans Family lived in Apartment 17C of the Cabrini Housing Project in Chicago. What was their monthly rent?

Q285. Florida, the mother, had to take a job to support the family after her husband, James, was killed in a car accident after the second TV season. For whom did Florida work?

Gilligan's Island

A279. Bruce

A280. 79 degrees

A281. "Miss Hourglass" ("They said I had all the sand in the right places.")

A282. "The Rain Dancers of Rango Rango" or "Belly Dancers From Bali Bali"

A283. Five different mutations of ragweed

Good Times

A284. $104

A285. Roadway Bus Company

Good Times continued

Q286. Resourceful, bop-talking J.J. was the oldest child and a hopeful artist. Before working for a greeting card company, J.J. held a job at what fast-food place?

Q287. "Buffalo Butt" was the name J.J. and neighbor Willona called Nathan Bookman, the building's overweight janitor. Of what fraternity was Nathan a member?

Green Acres
CBS, 1965–71

Q288. Lisa and Oliver Douglas traded in their life of luxury on Park Avenue to become farmers in the small town of Hooterville. Their new digs, a rather decrepit house, was actually a local landmark—the birthplace of "the founder of the great state of Hooterville." Who founded Hooterville?

Q289. Probably the only farmer in the world who did his chores wearing a suit and tie, Oliver was also most likely the only one to plow his fields with an ancient, broken-down tractor. What make of tractor did Oliver own?

Q290. Handyman Eb Dawson constantly called Oliver "Dad" even though they were not related. Eb sort of came with the farm and had a poster of his hero on his bedroom wall. What Western movie star was Eb's hero?

Q291. Although he was a pig, his official name was Arnold Ziffel. Arnold attended third grade, liked lime soda, and played cricket. He also had a favorite TV show. What was it?

Growing Pains
ABC, 1988–92

Q292. Jason and Maggie Seaver, a professional couple with four children (Mike, Carol, Ben and Chrissy), lived in Huntington, New York. The Seavers' garbage was picked up on Tuesdays and Fridays by whom?

A286. Chicken Shack

A287. The Jolly Janitors Club

Green Acres

A288. Rutherford B. Skrugg

A289. Hoyt-Clagwell

A290. Hoot Gibson

A291. *The CBS Evening News With Walter Cronkite*

Growing Pains

A292. Municipal Removal Service

Growing Pains continued

Q293. Jason was a psychologist who left his job at a hospital to open a private practice from his home. Where did Jason initially work?

Q294. Maggie majored in journalism and for two years was a researcher for *Newsweek* magazine before giving up her career to raise a family. When Jason set up his practice at home, Maggie returned to work. For what paper did she become a reporter?

Q295. Oldest child Mike was the number-one problem student at school, and it seemed highly unlikely that he would become a teacher, but he did. Prior to this he was an aspiring actor. On what TV show did Mike make his acting debut?

Q296. Carol, the older daughter, attended Dewey High School and Columbia University. She was studying law and took what subway train to get to school?

Q297. Benjamin Hubert Humphrey Seaver was the third born. He attended Wendell Willkie Elementary School and had an imaginary friend. What was the friend's name?

Q298. Chrissy, the youngest, was born at 12:30 A.M. and weighed eight pounds four ounces. Her favorite story was "Mr. Mouse," and she had several plush toys—a whale, a bear, and a pig. She called the pig "Papa Pig." What did she call the whale and bear?

Happy Days
ABC, 1974–84

Q299. Life in the 1950s was depicted through the experiences of the Cunningham family: parents Howard and Marion and their children Richie and Joanie. Howard owned the Cunningham Hardware Store. What service did he offer?

Q300. When Howard first went into a certain hardware store and saw the shelves lined with goods, he was hooked. He became a stockboy and by 1946 he owned the place. From what supplier did Howard get his goods?

A293.   Long Island General Hospital

A294.   *Long Island Daily Herald*

A295.   *New York Heat*

A296.   The Number One I.R.T.

A297.   Pirate Pete

A298.   The whale was Mr. Blow Hole; the bear was Bertha Big Jeans

Happy Days

A299.   Free paint color-mixing

A300.   Ernie's Hardware Store

Happy Days continued

Q301. Richie was called "Freckles" as a kid (age nine) and was said to resemble Howdy Doody. Meat loaf was his favorite dinner, but what was his favorite breakfast?

Q302. It had the license plate number F-7193 and it was Richie's first car, a 1952 Ford. What did he call the car?

Q303. Joanie, Richie's sister, was fondly called "Shortcake" and "Pumpkin." She was a member of the Junior Chipmunks Scout Troop and attended Jefferson High School. As anyone knows who watched the show, Howard was always talking about something that became Joanie's first word as a baby. What was her first word?

Q304. While Richie's favorite meal was meat loaf, Joanie preferred something totally different. What was it?

Q305. Arthur Herbert Fonzarelli, better known as "The Fonz" or "Fonzie," was the cool, leather-jacketed high school dropout admired by everyone. The Fonz had a bathrobe that said "Sweetums" ("Hey, it was a gift from a girl") and he used what brand of after-shave lotion?

Q306. While Fonzie seemed to have almost everything, including any girl he wanted, he was plagued by "The Fonzarelli Curse." What was it?

Q307. Boy-crazy Jenny Piccolo, Joanie's best friend, called herself "the object of mad desire." Jenny was not as busty as she would have liked to be. What did she order to make herself "more of a sexpot than I already am?"

Q308. Arnold's Drive-In was the famous after-school hangout. Fonzie's "offices" were in the "Guy's Room," and there was a soda machine near the front door. What brand did it dispense?

A301. Blueberry pancakes and fresh-squeezed orange juice

A302. The Love Bandit

A303. "Hardware"

A304. Baked macaroni and apple sauce

A305. Mr. Musk

A306. "When I'm asked to be best man at a wedding, disaster happens."

A307. The Ajax Bust Developer

A308. Spring Time Cola

Hazel
NBC/CBS, 1961–66

Q309. "Who's the gal who's everybody's pal, it's Hazel; she's the one who can make the sun begin to glow..." Thus goes the theme to this now classic TV series. Hazel was the maid to the Baxters: George, Dorothy, and son, Harold. She was the all-around problem solver and a member of what society of maids?

Q310. Hazel's insurance policy covered her back when she bowled, and she was famous for her fudge brownies. She also owned eleven shares of stock in what company?

Q311. George said that "Hazel will never tell a lie; she has George Washington heroics." He also declared that Hazel was the only person who knew the true meaning of Christmas. Why?

Q312. Hazel served breakfast at seven o'clock, lunch at 12:15, and dinner at 6:30. She took time off to attend mass on Sunday and had one day a week off. What day was it?

Q313. George, a lawyer, attended Dartmouth, was a member of the board of regents of the university law school, and began practicing in 1949. Name the firm for which George worked (and was a partner).

Q314. George was particularly fond of Hazel's fudge brownies. What did he call them?

Q315. Dorothy, a free-lance interior decorator, bought her dresses at Monteque's Boutique. Where did she buy her lingerie?

Q316. Herbert and Harriet Johnson were the Baxters' elderly neighbors and George's clients. Herbert was a retired investor who cornered the market on whale bones. How many whale bones did he have?

Q317. In the last-season episodes, Hazel became the maid to George's younger brother, Steve, his wife, Barbara, and their daughter, Susie. Hazel and Barbara attempted to make money by marketing a chili sauce created by Hazel. What did they call the product?

Hazel

A309.   The Sunshine Girls

A310.   The Davidson Vacuum Cleaner Company

A311.   She makes her own presents.

A312.   Thursday

A313.   Butterworth, Hatch, Noll, and Baxter

A314.   Hazel's Peachy Keen Pecan Brownies

A315.   Blackstone's Department Store

A316.   427 tons

A317.   Aunt Hazel's Chili Sauce

Head of the Class
ABC, 1986–91

Q318. Before becoming a teacher at Fillmore High School, Charlie Moore was an actor who appeared in plays by Chekhov and Ibsen and directed the Off-Broadway play *The Little Shop of Horrors*. He also was in an Off-Broadway production of *Hair* and considered it to be his most embarrassing moment. Why?

Q319. Before leaving Fillmore to star in the road production of *Death of a Salesman*, Charlie worked as the "King of Discount Appliances" for what company?

Q320. Billy MacGregor replaced Charlie as the history teacher for the I.H.P. (Individual Honors Program) students. Billy was from Scotland and took a second job shortly after joining the Fillmore staff. Where was it?

Q321. Bernadette Meara, the assistant principal, was born in North Carolina and came to New York in 1974 for the job. She enjoyed the Christmas holidays, but when she was seven, she experienced the saddest Christmas of her life. What happened?

Q322. Simone was the prettiest girl in the Honors Program. Her specialty was English and she had a romantic vision of life. She also was a member of the chess club, but lost all her femininity in the class. Why?

Q323. Wealthy Darlene believed she was very attractive to men ("I represent the physical and intellectual ideals men want"). She was also a descendant of which historically famous black woman?

Q324. Arvid had a perfect attendance record. Nothing stopped him—not blizzards, hurricanes, subway strikes, or illness. How many days of school had Arvid logged by October 1990?

Q325. Arvid played triangle in the school orchestra, was the lunchroom monitor, and admired writer Carl Sagan. When he got upset, he opened his wallet and talked to a picture of what famous person?

Head of the Class

A318.   He did the nude scene in the wrong act.

A319.   Veemer Appliances

A320.   The Mother Hubbard Day Care Center

A321.   She didn't get a Susie Q Easy Bake Oven.

A322.   The teacher called her "Mister."

A323.   Sally Hemmings, by whom Thomas Jefferson had children.

A324.   2,252

A325.   Albert Einstein

Head of the Class continued

Q326. Dennis was skilled in chemistry and physics, but was also the practical-joke player among his classmates. His antics got him sent to the principal's office so many times that he lost count. While waiting to be scolded, what did he do?

Q327. The I.H.P. classes were held in Room 19, where there was a Rand-McNally map on the wall and two computers. What did the kids call the computers?

Home Improvement
ABC, 1991–

Q328. Tim Taylor is the host of a comical home improvement show in Detroit. His wife, Jill, complains most often that he leaves the cap off the toothpaste tube. On the show, Tim is assisted by Al, who also carps about the things Tim forgets to do, like leaving the cap off what?

Q329. While Tim may be boss of his garage workshop, Jill is the boss of the kitchen. She has two sponges and what specific rules for them?

Q330. Tim is obsessed with tools, especially those made by the show's sponsor, Binford Tools, and likes to shop for them. Where is he considered a valued customer?

The Honeymooners
CBS, 1955–56

Q331. He promised Alice the moon, but he was rarely able to provide any luxuries for her. Ralph Kramden was a bus driver ˋand earned $60 a week, but in 1955 it never seemed enough, and he ventured into many money-making schemes that all failed. He tried to market the Handy Housewife Helper on TV (as "The Chef of the Future") and he attempted low-cal pizza and glow-in-the-dark wallpaper (to cut down on electric bills). But he was most famous for investing in something. What was it?

A326. Stared at a picture of George Washington that is on the wall.

A327. Fred and Wilma

Home Improvement

A328. The epoxy glue tube

A329. The blue sponge is for the sink; the green sponge is for the counter

A330. Damon's Hardware Store

The Honeymooners

A331. A uranium mine in Asbury Park

The Honeymooners continued

Q332. Ralph and Alice had few electrical appliances, and their typical gas bill was thirty-nine cents a month. Still, to supplement their income, Alice took a job as a jelly donut stuffer at what bakery?

Q333. Edward L. Norton and his wife, Trixie, were the Kramdens' upstairs neighbors. Ed majored in arithmetic at vocational school and now works in sewers. As a kid he had a dog named Lulu and mentioned that the "L" in his name stood for what?

Q334. Ed and Ralph were members of the Raccoon Lodge and also bowled on the same team. What was the team's name?

Q335. To become a lodge member, one had to have a public school diploma, be a resident of the United States for at least six months, and pay a $1.50 initiation fee. The most expensive aspect of being a member was the cost of the uniform. How much was it?

I Love Lucy
CBS, 1951–57

Q336. Fred and Ethel Mertz were the owners of the Manhattan brownstone that was home to bandleader Ricky Ricardo and his scatterbrained wife, Lucy. The Ricardos lived in Apartment 3B and paid how much a month rent?

Q337. Lucy was born in Jamestown, New York. When she attended grade school what did the kids call her?

Q338. At Jamestown High, Lucy was Juliet in the school's production of *Romeo and Juliet* and was a member of the band. She played the saxophone but only learned one song. What was it?

Q339. Perhaps one of the most famous episodes in the series was the one in which Lucy becomes intoxicated while doing a commercial for Vitameatavegamin, a vitamin product with a 32 percent alcohol content. But what program was the commercial for?

A332.   Krausmeyer's

A333.   Lilywhite (his mother's maiden name)

A334.   The Hurricanes

A335. $35

I Love Lucy

A336. $125

A337.   "Bird Legs"

A338.   "Glow Worm"

A339.   *Your Saturday Night Variety Show*

I Love Lucy continued

Q340. Lucy's goal was to break into show business despite Ricky's objections. While it was not a glitzy dance number in one of Ricky's shows, "Breakfast with Lucy and Ricky" made Lucy a TV star when she cohosted it. What company sponsored the show?

Q341. Lucy and Ricky became the parents of Little Ricky in 1953. The youngster had a number of pets, including a dog, two fish, two parakeets, two turtles, and a frog. Little Ricky called the frog Hopalong and the dog Fred. What were the names of either the fish or parakeets?

Q342. Ricky's most annoying habit, according to Lucy, was tapping his fingers. What did Ricky say was Lucy's most annoying habit?

Q343. Ethel claimed that Fred's habit of jingling his keys was most annoying to her, but what did Fred say Ethel's most annoying habit was?

I Married Joan
NBC, 1952–55

Q344. Joan Stevens called herself "a real goof; a girl who is guaranteed to foul things up." Married to Judge Bradley Stevens, Joan tried hard to be a good housewife and was good at maneuvering the household funds to balance the budget. She couldn't, though, resist shopping for bargains. What did the salesmen call her?

Q345. A member of the Women's Welfare League, Joan considered herself to be very popular. She was a Guy Lombardo fan and loved TV soap operas. What was the title of her favorite one?

Q346. Brad called Joan "Lover" and liked to hear the words "Dinner is ready." What was his favorite meal?

Q347. A domestic relations judge, Brad enjoyed two hobbies. One was hunting. What was the other one?

A340. Phipps Drug Store

A341. Alice and Phil (parakeets); Mildred and Charles (fish)

A342. Hitting the spoon against the side of a cup while stirring coffee.

A343. "Chewing like a cow."

I Married Joan

A344. "One of those yo-yo dames."

A345. *Two Hearts Against the World*

A346. Pot roast

A347. Stamp collecting

The Jack Benny Program
CBS/NBC, 1950–65

Q348. He had been thirty-nine for so long that Jack Benny had forgotten how old he really was. He also claimed that his writers were responsible for the image people had of him as being cheap. Jack had a vault in his basement, but he also had funds in the bank, and while he rarely withdrew money from the bank, he loved to visit it. What happened when Jack went to the bank?

Q349. Jack had a laundry business on the side and enjoyed attending parties, so much so that he was listed in the yellow pages. What did his listing say?

Q350. While Jack Benny actually could play the violin, he faked being a terrible violinist on the air. He also thought of himself as a songwriter. Name the awful song he composed.

Q351. Real-life wife Mary Livingstone was Jack's radio and TV girlfriend, a salesgirl at the May Company. Jack sometimes treated Mary to dinner (if he could find a cheap enough restaurant) and did take her on dates. However, what was Jack's idea of seeing a movie with Mary?

Just the Ten of Us
ABC, 1988–90

Q352. The Lubbocks were a family of ten residing in Eureka, California. Graham and Elizabeth were the parents, and their children were Marie, Wendy, Cindy, Connie, Sherry, J.R., and infant twins Michelle and Harvey. Graham was the football coach at St. Augie's. What was the name of the team?

Q353. Marie, Wendy, Connie, and Cindy formed a singing group called the Lubbock Babes. A big hit in Eureka, the girls performed regularly at what local eatery?

Q354. Seventeen-year-old Wendy was the prettiest of the girls. She was boy-crazy and wore a size 7½ shoe and a size 5 dress. Name one of the two shades of lipstick she wore.

The Jack Benny Program

A348. He caused a run on it.

A349. "Available for Parties"

A350. "When You Say I Beg Your Pardon, Then I'll Come Back to You"

A351. Going over to her house because the TV screen was bigger.

Just the Ten of Us

A352. The Hippos

A353. Danny's Pizza Parlor

A354. "Dawn at His Place" or "Midnight Passion"

Just the Ten of Us continued

Q355. Cindy was the not-too-bright Lubbock Babe. She was sixteen, had a slight weight problem, and her middle name was Anne. However, it was only late in the series that Cindy realized Anne was her middle name. What did she believe her middle name was?

Q356. Connie, the most intelligent of the children, was fifteen and also the most sensitive. She hoped to become a writer, but her first job was sweeping up animal entrails at what slaughterhouse?

Kate and Allie
CBS, 1984–88

Q357. We all know them as Kate and Allie, single mothers who shared a Manhattan apartment to save on expenses. They first met as kids at the orthodontist and each character had a full name. What were those names?

Q358. Kate worked while Allie cared for her children, Jennie and Chip, and Kate's daughter, Emma. For what company did Kate work, and at what school did Allie take night classes?

Q359. Whether it was Christmas or a birthday, Kate and Allie always exchanged the same gifts. Allie gave Kate a purse. What did Kate give Allie?

Q360. In 1988 Allie married Bob Barsky, a famous football player turned TV sportscaster. For what station did Bob work?

Laverne and Shirley
ABC, 1976–83

Q361. Laverne DeFazio and Shirley Feeney, blue-collar friends who shared an apartment in Milwaukee during the 1960s, shopped at Slotnick's Supermarket, and worked in the bottle-capping division of the Shotz Brewery. When the girls served a hitch in the army, Shirley wrote of their experiences under what pen name?

A355.   Diane

A356.   MacGregor's

Kate and Allie

A357.   Kate was Katherine Elizabeth Ann McArdle; Allie was Allison Julie Charlotte Adams Lowell.

A358.   Kate worked for the Sloane Travel Agency; Allie attended Washington Square College.

A359.   A sweater

A360.   WNTD, Channel 10

Laverne and Shirley

A361.   S. Wilhelmina Feeney

Laverne and Shirley continued

Q362. Laverne suffered from claustrophobia, and milk and Pepsi was her favorite drink. What was her favorite sandwich?

Q363. Shirley had a plush cat named Boo Boo Kitty and was famous for the Shirley Feeney Scarf Dance. What was the one food Shirley would not order with extra barbecue sauce ("It's messy and gets under my nails")?

Q364. Lenny and Squiggy were Laverne and Shirley's friends, although they didn't like that to be known by too many people. Lenny enjoyed horror movies and sports, but as a kid he had only what one "toy" to play with?

Q365. Squiggy was most proud of his moth collection and had been blessed with the family birthmark. What was it?

Q366. When the series switched locales to California, Lenny and Squiggy became ice cream vendors and talent agents. To meet young starlets they wrote a horror movie. What was it called?

Leave It to Beaver
CBS/ABC, 1957–62

Q367. The Cleavers—Ward and June and young sons Wally and Beaver—lived at 211 Pine Street in the town of Mayfield. Ward, who grew up on Shaker Avenue and was an engineer with the Seabees during World War II, enjoyed fishing and reading the daily newspaper. What was the paper's name?

Q368. Wally was a three-letter man at Mayfield High School whose best time as a member of the swimming team was 53.2 seconds. He also played varsity football and wore what brand of after-shave lotion?

Q369. Younger brother Beaver had the real first name of Theodore. Whom was Theodore named after?

A362. Peanut butter and sauerkraut on raisin bread

A363. Chicken

A364. Sauerkraut

A365. A red blotch shaped like Abraham Lincoln.

A366. *Blood Orgy of the Amazon*

Leave It to Beaver

A367. *The Mayfield Press*

A368. Arabian Knights

A369. June's Aunt Martha's brother

Leave It to Beaver continued

Q370. Beaver wasn't much for mushy stuff and liked to "mess around with junk." He hated girls but loved fishing. Where did he fish?

Q371. Wally's friend, Eddie Haskell, was overly polite to adults but mean to everybody else, especially Beaver, whom he called "Squirt." He also used three nicknames for Wally. Name two of them.

Q372. The wisecracking Eddie was also the first of Wally's buddies to get a credit card. To show off, he also misused it. What outfit issued Eddie a card?

Q373. Ward's occupation was never revealed, although it appeared he may have been an accountant. At any rate, he worked for Fred Rutherford. What did Fred call Ward?

Love and War
CBS, 1992–95

Q374. The Blue Shamrock, a Manhattan bar owned by Wally Porter, was frequented by Jack Stein, Mary Margaret Tynan, and Ray Litvak. Before purchasing the place Wally owned a classy uptown restaurant on East 72nd Street. What was it called?

Q375. Wally is a renowned gourmet cook. She can serve twelve dinners in twenty-one minutes and debone a chicken in how many seconds?

Q376. Kip Zakaris is Wally's ex-husband, an impossibly vain actor who appeared Off-Broadway in *West Side Story* (playing Jet #2); on TV's *Lou Grant* (a deranged typesetter); and in what often mentioned pilot "about a meat inspector who drives a Ferrari"?

Q377. Newspaper columnist Jack Stein, Wally's romantic interest, won an award for a story on illiteracy. What is the name of his column?

A370.   Miller's Lake

A371.   "Sam," "Gertrude," or "Ellwood"

A372.   Universal Gas and Oil Company

A373.   "Lord of the Manor"

Love and War

A374.   The Chez Wally Restaurant

A375.   Twenty

A376.   "Turf and Surf"

A377.   "The Steinway"

Love That Bob
NBC/CBS, 1955–59

Q378. Bob Collins was a swinging young bachelor who owned a photography studio in Hollywood. A confirmed bachelor, he needed time to find the right girl—"no matter how many girls I have to date to find her." Bob simply could not resist a beautiful woman and wore what cologne that drove them crazy?

Q379. Bob may have worked long hours but he rarely complained when it came to photographing beautiful models. However, he insisted that his swimsuit models could not have a waist larger than what size?

Q380. "The Casanova of the camera," as his sister Margaret called him, found which month of the year the most difficult in which to stay single?

Q381. Some of the most beautiful women in movies appeared on *Love That Bob*, including blond Joi Lansing as Shirley Swanson, a model who was determined to marry Bob. She took no chances, and even her perfume spelled trouble for him. What perfume did Shirley wear?

Mad About You
NBC, 1992–

Q382. Paul and Jamie are the married couple mad about each other. They live in Manhattan and have a dog named Murray. Paul, born in New York City and a graduate of NYU Film School, now runs his own documentary film company. What does he call it?

Q383. Jamie was born in Connecticut and attended Yale University. She likes to be liked by people, and when she feels someone she would like to know doesn't like her, she goes to extremes—as in high school when she did something to impress a boy. Because of what she did, she got a reputation. What was she called?

Love That Bob

A378. Moustache

A379. 23 inches

A380. June—when girls are the most marriage-minded.

A381. "Bachelor's Doom"

Mad About You

A382. Buchman Films

A383. "The Stemple sister who showed a boy her boobs to be liked."

Madame's Place
Syndicated, 1982–83

Q384. Madame, the hand puppet of Wayland Flowers, was the host of *Madame's Place*, a late night talk show that broadcast from her Beverly Hills mansion. She began her career as a comedienne in dingy clubs but hit the big time in movies, and starred with Clint Eastwood in what mythical movie of which she was most proud?

Q385. Madame read the *Enquiring Star* and was a member of the Fetish of the Month Club. What brand of body rubbing oil did she order?

Q386. Sara Joy Pitts was Madame's ultrasexy niece, coming to Hollywood from Georgia to be an actress "like my auntie Madame." Not-too-bright Sara Joy watched what favorite TV soap opera with the sound off "because it's so sad and it makes me cry"?

Q387. A former "two-bit band singer," Lynn LaVecque went on to host a show that is aired opposite *Madame's Place*. What was the name of Lynn's show that was costing Madame viewers.

Major Dad
CBS, 1989–93

Q388. John MacGillis was a tough marine who married a widow (Polly) with three daughters (Elizabeth, Robin, and Casey). He was born in Mississippi, where his grandfather taught him to whittle and where, at the age of seven, he made the biggest mistake of his life. What was it?

Q389. John was originally stationed in Oceanside, California, then in Furlough, Virginia, where he was the aide to Gen. Marcus Craig. What was the nickname for the job John held?

Q390. In California, Polly was a reporter for the *Oceanside Chronicle*. For what paper did she work when the family moved to Virginia?

Madame's Place

A384. *A Woman Named Hey You*

A385. "Me Tarzan—You Jane"

A386. *The Young and the Stupid*

A387. *Naked All-Star Bowling*

Major Dad

A388. He stole a Zorro wristwatch that cost $7.95.

A389. "Staff Weenie"

A390. Writer for the camp newspaper, *The Bulldog*

Major Dad *continued*

Q391. Teenage Elizabeth was the prettiest of the girls, but was somewhat embarrassed when looking through the family photo album. Why?

Q392. Sister Robin was the tomboy of the family. In California she was a member of the school's basketball team, the Condors. In Virginia she was in the girls' softball league. What was the name of her team?

Q393. Casey, the youngest, had two dolls, a bird, and a teddy bear. Lemon was the name of the bird, and Ruby and Henrietta were the dolls. What did Casey call her teddy bear?

Q394. Alva Lou Bricker, nicknamed "Gunny," was General Craig's administrative chief. She referred to Casey as "Little Cooper," and she herself had a dog. What did she call it?

Q395. When Marcus Craig, the commanding officer of Camp Hollister, got upset, he went to the firing range to shoot off several hundred rounds. He was often upset by his wife who, although never seen, was constantly mentioned. What was her name?

Mama's Family
NBC, 1983–84

Q396. The Harpers were a not-so-typical family living in the mythical Raytown, U.S.A. Thelma "Mama" Harper was the cantankerous head of the family. Her street address was now 1542 Ray Way, but many years ago it had been 10 Decatur Road, at which time it was a brothel. What was the brothel called?

Q397. Mama wore a perfume called "Obsession" and she was a member of the Raytown Community Church League. She was also most secretive about the ingredients in what favorite recipe?

A391.   She worried about how her hair looked.

A392.   The Hollister Hornets

A393.   Mr. Smithers

A394.   Elmo

A395.   Mimsey

Mama's Family

A396.   Ma Beaudien's

A397.   Million dollar fudge

Mama's Family continued

Q398. Mama's son, Vinton, was married to Naomi and owned a twenty-five-year collection of *TV Guide*. His favorite watering hole was the Bigger Jigger Bar and he was a member of what fraternity?

Q399. Mama believed Naomi to be the kind of girl mothers fear their sons will marry. Naomi had four previous marriages and worked at what local supermarket?

Q400. Spinster Iola Bolen was Mama's longtime friend. She enjoyed arts and crafts and lived with her own domineering mother. Iola envisioned herself as an actress and performed with what local theater group?

Married...With Children
Fox, 1987–

Q401. Al Bundy is a shoe salesman. As we all know, his wife, Peggy, claims it is the most demeaning, low-paying job there is. What is Al's yearly salary?

Q402. Al has an obsession with "hooters" as he calls them and loves watching such classic films as *Planet of the D Cups* and *Breast Monsters From Venus*. A copy of Al's favorite girlie magazine can be found around the house. What is it?

Q403. The family rarely gets a decent meal because Peggy doesn't shop for food or know that "that big white hot thing in the kitchen" is a stove. For Thanksgiving they have a Bundy turkey (a pizza) and on Labor Day, Bundy Burgers. Exactly what are Bundy Burgers?

Q404. Peggy was born in Wanker County and spends her days watching TV and eating bonbons. She avoids work (around or out of the house) and also refuses to do something that will make Al happy for once in his life. What is it?

A398.   Mystic Order of the Cobra Lodge

A399.   Food Circus

A400.   Peppermint Playhouse Theater Company

Married...with Children

A401. $12,000

A402.   *Biggums*

A403.   Last year's grease and ashes for this year's burgers

A404.   Leave him

Married... With Children continued

Q405. "I was born in February. I'm an aquarium," says Kelly, the mall-shopping Bundy daughter. She had a job as a model representing one of Al's favorite foods (hot dogs wrapped in bread and fried in lard). What title did Kelly hold?

Q406. When needing $400 to enroll in modelling school, Kelly pouted and inveigled money from Al. The course paid off as it got her several jobs, but there was a drawback—she got tension headaches from smiling. Kelly was told, though, she was a natural—a natural at what?

Q407. Kelly calls him "Rat Boy" and "Toad Boy," but Bud, her younger brother, believes he is a ladies' man—despite the laughs from Al and Peggy. When Bud can't get a date, he watches what TV show?

Q408. Bud calls his cowboy pajamas his "love clothes" and Kelly claims that he watches *Star Trek* reruns "to get a glimpse of Klingon cleavage." In an attempt to get girls, Bud has pretended to be a street rapper. What did he call himself?

The Mary Tyler Moore Show
CBS, 1970–77

Q409. Thirty and single, Mary Richards worked as the associate producer of the Channel 12 *Six O'Clock News* in Minneapolis, hired by the show's producer, Lou Grant, because she had spunk "and a nice caboose." While Lou did like Mary's physical features, he hated something about her. What was it?

Q410. Lou played college football and was a distinguished newsman before his job as a news producer. Like clockwork, something came to his office on the fifteenth of each month. What was it?

Q411. Ted Baxter, the station's incompetent newscaster, yearned for a job in New York City with his hero, Walter Cronkite. Despite the grumblings from the news staff, Ted was paid a lot more than they received. What was his yearly salary?

A405.   "Miss Weenie Tots"

A406.   Leg crossing ("I can do it at will.")

A407.   *Dateless Dude Late Night Theater*

A408.   Grand Master B.

The Mary Tyler Moore Show

A409.   Her parties ("You give rotten parties. I've had some of the worst times of my life at your parties.")

A410.   His bar bill

A411. $31,000

The Mary Tyler Moore Show continued

Q412. Rhoda Morganstern, Mary's best friend and upstairs neighbor, moved to Minneapolis when she couldn't find a job or an apartment in New York. A window dresser at Hempell's Department Store, Rhoda had a pet goldfish. What did she call it?

Q413. Shortly after first arriving in Minneapolis, Rhoda went to the zoo, where she was fined $40 for feeding a buffalo. What did she give it?

M*A*S*H
CBS, 1972–83

Q414. Col. Henry Blake was the initial commanding officer of the 4077th M*A*S*H unit in Korea, and loved fishing and clowning around with subordinate officers Hawkeye and Trapper John. From what company did Henry order girlie films for his men?

Q415. Col. Sherman Potter, who replaced Henry as the commanding officer, was born in Missouri and loved horses. Stricter than Henry, he had made the army his career. For doing so, his wife had a nickname for him. What was it?

Q416. Capt. Benjamin Franklin Pierce, better known as "Hawkeye," was drafted, and by defying authority, fought back at the system. He called the unit a cesspool and would not carry a gun. He had a still in his tent and enjoyed reading what magazine?

Q417. Corp. Maxwell Klinger was the unit's resident loon, pretending to be crazy by dressing as a woman to get a Section 8 discharge. While waiting in vain for it to happen, Klinger started a camp newspaper. What did he call it?

Q418. Radar O'Reilly was the company clerk and had the ability to perceive what others think. He also had a number of pets: Moe, Jack, Babette, and Margo (guinea pigs); Fluffy and Bingo (rabbits); and a mouse. What did he call the mouse?

A412.   Goldfish

A413.   Yogurt

M*A*S*H

A414.   Tabasco Films

A415.   "Puddin' Head"

A416.   *The Joys of Nudity*

A417.   "M*A*S*H Notes"

A418.   Daisy

*M*A*S*H continued*

Q419. While Hawkeye had his own source for martinis, he also frequented the local watering hole. What was it called?

Mork and Mindy
ABC, 1978–82

Q420. Ork was a planet with three moons whose inhabitants resembled humans but evolved from the chicken. How far from Earth was Ork?

Q421. Orson, a planet leader, assigned Mork to be an Earth Observer and to report to him on Earth activities. What were Mork's telepathic reports to Orson called?

Q422. Mork took up residence with an Earth girl named Mindy McConnell in Boulder, Colorado. Mindy first worked in her father's music store, then as a newscaster at what TV station?

Q423. After Mork and Mindy married (1981), Mork laid an egg that hatched and produced an adult male son they named Mearth (Orkan children are born old and grow younger with time). Mearth attended Ork Prep School one day a month via the Orkan school bus. What was this bus?

Q424. Exidor was the local loon, a fanatic who believed in taking up causes; unfortunately, he did it in all the wrong ways. Brutus was Exidor's invisible dog, but what was the name of his invisible aide?

Mr. Belvedere
ABC, 1985–90

Q425. Lynn Belvedere had appeared on the cover of *World Focus* magazine, had climbed Mount Everest, and had even won the Pillsbury Bake-Off. He had served royalty but now worked as the housekeeper to the Owens, a chaotic family of five in Pittsburgh. At the end of each episode Lynn was seen writing his day's activities in his diary. Name the book he planned to turn his diary into.

A419.   Rosie's Bar

Mork and Mindy

A420.   200 million miles

A421.   The Scorpio Reports

A422.   KTNS, Channel 31

A423.   The 828 Transport Beam

A424.   Pepe

Mr. Belvedere

A425.   *An American Journal: The Suburban Years*

Mr. Belvedere continued

Q426. The Owens family consisted of parents George and Marsha and children Kevin, Heather, and Wesley. George originally hosted "Sports Page" on an AM radio station and he later became the sportscaster for what program on Channel 8?

Q427. Marsha was originally a law student and passed the bar in 1987. With what company did she find work?

Q428. Kevin was the oldest of the children. He attended Van Buren High School and worked part time after school at what fast food store?

Q429. In the middle was Heather, popular at school and with a girlfriend named Angela. Angela was a bit kooky, "and being blonde and pretty are about all Angela has going for her," said Heather. Angela couldn't remember Mr. Belvedere's name (she called him, for example, "Mr. Bell Bottoms" or "Mr. Belly Buster"). What did Angela collect?

Q430. Wesley, the youngest and most mischievous of the Owens children, was a member of the Colts Little League Team and had two pets: a dog and a snake. The dog was Spot; what was the snake's name?

The Munsters
CBS, 1964–66

Q431. The run-down house at 1313 Mockingbird Lane was the residence of the Munster family—parents Herman and Lily, son Eddie, niece Marilyn, and Lily's father, Grandpa. Herman, who resembled Frankenstein, was 150 years old and a gravedigger for Gateman, Goodbury, and Graves. Herman "attended" medical school for six years in several jars. What was the name of the school?

Q432. Herman was over seven feet tall, weighed three spins on the bathroom scale, had a ham radio, and wrote poetry for the company magazine, which published his first poem, "Going Out to Pasture." What was the magazine called?

A426. "Metro News"

A427. The Legal Hut

A428. Mr. Cluck's Fried Chicken

A429. Hangers

A430. Captain Nemo

The Munsters

A431. The Heidelberg School of Medicine

A432. *The Mortician's Monthly*

The Munsters continued

Q433. When Herman had a medical exam, the following was revealed: heartbeat none; pulse 15; blood pressure minus three; and what body temperature?

Q434. Lily's maiden name was Dracula. She was 304 years old and her favorite food was bat milk yogurt. Lily did work for what pet charity?

Q435. Grandpa, Lily's father, was an admitted mad scientist, with a lab in the dungeon beneath the Munster Mansion. His favorite TV show was *My Three Sons*. He also had a transistorized divining rod that rarely worked because it picked up the reruns of what old television series?

Q436. The family pet was Spot, a fire-breathing dragon Grandpa found while digging up the backyard. What brand of dog food did Lily feed Spot?

The Munsters Today
Syndicated, 1988–91

Q437. This update of the 1964–66 series *The Munsters* kept most of the aspects of the original show although some changes were made. Herman was now said to be over three hundred years old and worked for Mr. Graves (not Mr. Gateman). As in the original series, Herman was made from a number of different parts, including the muscles of Count Schwarzenegger, the right arm of Igor Johnson (a pickpocket), and the nose of Gregory Fabrock. Who was Gregory Fabrock?

Q438. When Herman felt that the time had come to open his own funeral parlor, he quit his day job and purchased a bankrupt donut shop. What did he call his business?

Q439. Lily was now 324 years old and has been married to Herman for 299 years. Where did Lily work before they wed?

A433.   62.8 degrees

A434.   Bundles for Transylvania

A435.   *My Little Margie*

A436.   Doggie's Din Din

The Munsters Today

A437.   The village idiot

A438.   The House of Herman

A439.   As a singer at Club Dead

The Munsters Today continued

Q440.   Grandpa was still a mad scientist and Igor still his pet bat. But there was now another resident in the dungeon, a skeleton he befriended in college. Name it.

Q441.   Marilyn was a college student in the original series, but a high schooler here. While the 1964 Marilyn had no problem with dates (it was one look at Herman that scared them off), the 1988 Marilyn desperately wants a bigger bosom to attract boys. What size did she want to be?

Q442.   Grave Diggers Mutual, "The Good Hands People," insured the Munster home at 1313 Mockingbird Lane and something else the family owned at 13-13th Avenue. What was it?

Murphy Brown
CBS, 1988–

Q443.   A behind-the-scenes look at the preparations that go into making a TV newsmagazine (*F.Y.I.*) is the basis for this series. The Museum of Broadcast Arts and Sciences awarded *F.Y.I.* with what honor?

Q444.   Murphy Brown is a hard-hitting investigative reporter who has a reputation for getting even with anyone who crosses her. But she does have a caring side ("I once fed the cat next door"), although people say she could never take care of a pet. Murphy, though, says she has. What kind of "pet" was it?

Q445.   Aretha Franklin is Murphy's favorite singer; "Respect" is her favorite song, and she is fond of what particular type of flower?

Q446.   Corky Sherwood is a reporter who can recite all the books of the Bible by heart. She was crowned Miss America at age nineteen, does stories like "Woody Woodpecker's 50th Birthday," and conducts interviews with "people" such as the San Diego chicken. In 1989 she won the Humboldt News Award for which one of her stories?

A440.   Leonard

A441.   36D

A442.   Munster Moor

Murphy Brown

A443.   Fifteen Years of Excellence in Journalism

A444.   "I got a Chia Pet to grow."

A445.   Sterling roses

A446.   "A Woman's Touch at West Point"

Murphy Brown *continued*

Q447. Frank Fontana joined *F.Y.I.* in 1977. He attended the Bishop Fallon High School for Boys and was a reporter for the *New York Times* before *F.Y.I.* Despite all his hard work, how does *TV Guide* have a tendency to list him?

Q448. Jim Dial is the respected if rather uptight senior anchor of *F.Y.I.* His TV career didn't begin with news but as the host of a local Channel 9 kid show. What was it called?

Q449. Elden Berneke, Murphy's personal house painter and nanny for her son, Avery, uses Murphy's good pantyhose to strain paint and buys his supplies at Ed's Paints. What is his favorite watering hole?

Q450. Phil's Bar, established in 1919, is the *F.Y.I.* gang's regular eatery. Murphy's favorite meal there is what?

My Living Doll
CBS, 1964–65

Q451. Dr. Carl Miller created AF 709, a beautiful female cyborg, for a project designed to send robots into outer space. Before it began, she was given to Bob McDonald, a psychologist, to mold her character, and he named her Rhoda while she posed as Carl's niece. Light provided Rhoda with power while her microsensors maintained her body temperature at 98.6 degrees. Where was her main power-off switch located?

Q452. Bob worked at the Cory Clinic where Rhoda posed as his secretary. Rhoda required no coffee breaks and could type how many words a minute?

My Mother the Car
NBC, 1965–66

Q453. Dave Crabtree was a lawyer whose dead mother had been reincarnated into the 1928 Porter he owned. What was his mother's first name?

A447. "Fred Fontana"

A448. *Poop Deck Pete and Cartoons Ahoy*

A449. The House Painter's Bar.

A450. A Phil Burger and Fries

My Living Doll

A451. On her right elbow

A452. 240

My Mother the Car

A453. Agatha

My Mother the Car continued

Q454. Dave paid $200 for the Porter, which still had its original brakes and carburetor. We could ask how many nuts, screws, and bolts did the carburetor have, but we won't. Instead, what brand of brakes did Mother have?

Q455. At night Dave covered Mother's radiator with a blanket so she wouldn't catch cold. He also bought her a used TV set (for $10) so she could watch her favorite TV show, which was what?

Q456. When Mother needed servicing, Dave would bring her to only one garage. Which one was it?

Newhart
CBS, 1982–90

Q457. Dick Loudon and his wife, Joanna, owned the Stratford Inn in Vermont. Joanna also sold real estate and Dick was a "How To" book author. After writing several such books, he decided to do one based on the inn. What did he call it?

Q458. Joanna and Bob also had TV shows on Channel 8. Bob hosted the daily program, *Vermont Today* and Joanna had a weekly real estate show that was originally called *Your House Is My House*. To improve ratings, what was it changed to?

Q459. George Utley, Dick's handyman, was a member of the Beaver Lodge and enjoyed bird watching at Johnny Kaye Lake. He also invented a board game. What did he call it?

Q460. A beautiful but quite spoiled and rather snooty heiress named Stephanie Vanderkellen took work as Dick's maid at the inn. She too had a series on Channel 8. What was it called?

Q461. Stephanie's boyfriend, Michael Harris, was the producer of her show. Insecure, he constantly showered her with gifts, but because there were not enough special holidays to give Stephanie presents, he created one (which comes between Valentine's Day and Easter). What day was it?

A454. Stops on a Dime Brakes. By the way, the carburetor had sixteen nuts, fourteen screws, and three bolts.

A455. *Jalopy Derby*

A456. Doc Benson's Auto Clinic

Newhart

A457. *Murder at the Stratley*

A458. *Hot Houses*

A459. Handyman: The Feel Good Game

A460. *Seein' Double*

A461. Cupcake Day

Newhart *continued*

Q462. The flounder was the town fish; the flying squirrel was the town bird. While the key to the city wouldn't open anything, it did do something. What?

Night Court
NBC, 1984–92

Q463. Harry Stone was a night-court arraignment judge in Manhattan. He was voted the Most Fascinating Judge in New York and was famous for his sentences. What were they?

Q464. Harry loved magic, was a Mel Torme fan, and had a specific coin as his lucky charm. What coin was it?

Q465. Christine Sullivan was the pretty legal aid attorney who said, "the most artistic people I get as clients are hookers with makeup skills." Easily exasperated, she often wondered why she became a lawyer. She had a car with Happy Face hubcaps and was a member of what support group?

Q466. Ian McKee was a New York street artist who found inspiration after meeting Christine. To show his gratitude, he painted a very large mural of her on a warehouse door. What did he call his masterpiece?

Q467. Ladies' man Dan Fielding earned his pay as a prosecuting attorney. He called his car "The Dan Mobile" and picked up girls at the Sticky Wickey. He also had a TV talk show. What was it called?

Q468. Dan Fielding was an assumed name. He was born on a rural farm in Louisiana and his parents named their kids and pigs after characters in books. What was Dan's real name?

Q469. Bull Shannon was the bald bailiff. He weighed 250 pounds and earned $320 a week. He got the nickname from his mother (she said "Bull" when she found out she was pregnant). What was Bull's real first name?

A462.   Start Willie Frye's tractor

Night Court

A463. $55 and time served

A464.   A Mercury-head dime

A465.   Ha Ha (Happy Alone, Happy Adults)

A466.   The Naked Body of Justice

A467.   *In Your Face*

A468.   Rheinhold Fielding Elmore

A469.   Nostradamus

Night Court *continued*

Q470. Bull lived next to a subway line in an apartment that had a concrete sofa ("durable, practical, and easy to patch") and a pet python. What was Bull's snake's name?

Q471. Roz Russell, the sassy bailiff, believed that her goal in life was to kick butt. But she didn't come by that belief in Harry's court; she learned it when she was a stewardess and encountered a group of annoying passengers. For what airline did Roz work?

Q472. Lisette was the pretty court stenographer who enjoyed knitting sweaters for birds, and also got a kick out of folding socks. She had a favorite lamp she called Sparky, a goldfish, and a plush giraffe. She called the giraffe Too Tall, but what did she call the goldfish?

The Odd Couple
ABC, 1970–74

Q473. Felix Unger was a neatnik; Oscar Madison a slob. They were divorced friends and roommates sharing an apartment in New York City. Nino's Italian Restaurant was their favorite eatery and they also managed to curtail their bickering long enough to write a song for singer Jaye P. Morgan. What did they call it?

Q474. Felix was born in Chicago, moved to Oklahoma, and grew up on a farm in upstate New York. He was a member of the Radio Actors Guild and in college had his own radio called *Felix*. On what real radio show did Felix appear as a kid?

Q475. During World War II, Felix was stationed in England and appeared in the army training film *How to Take a Shower* and originated the line "Men, don't let this happen to you." To what unit was he attached?

Q476. Felix also won the Silver Canteen Award during his service days for a song he wrote about Adolph Hitler. What was it called?

A470.   Bertha; later Harvey

A471.   Paramus Air Lines

A472.   Orca

The Odd Couple

A473.   "Happy and Peppy and Bursting With Love"

A474.   *Let's Pretend*

A475.   The 22nd Training Film Platoon, Educational Division of the Special Services

A476.   "To a Sour Kraut"

The Odd Couple *continued*

Q477. Gambling was Oscar's vice and Boston cream pie was his favorite dessert. While he did tend to put ketchup on everything, he also had a favorite dinner. What was it?

Q478. Oscar was born in Philadelphia at Our Lady of Angels Hospital. He attended the Langley Tippy-Toe Tap Dancing School as a kid and was enrolled in what high school?

One Day at a Time
CBS, 1975–84

Q479. The liberated Ann Romano and daughters Julie and Barbara resided at 1344 Hartford Drive in Indianapolis. Before owning her own ad agency, Ann worked for someone else. What was that company's name?

Q480. When Ann started her own agency, her first account was Startime Ice Cream. What was her biggest account at her previous job?

Q481. Julie, Ann's older and more troublesome daughter, had two favorite snacks. One was celery and ice cream. What was the other one?

Q482. Julie was rebellious, ran away from home, and wanted a career as a fashion designer. She never achieved her goal, but did find happiness when she married Max Horvath, a flight attendant who later tried his luck at writing. For what airline did Max work?

Q483. Younger sister Barbara attended Jefferson High School but dropped out of City College. She first worked for Quickie Burger, then at Olympic Sporting Goods, and finally at what travel agency?

Q484. The building super was Dwayne F. Schneider, a ladies' man who picked up girls at the Purple Pig Club. Dwayne's C.B. handle was "Super Stud" and he was a member of what lodge?

A477. Lasagna and French fries

A478. James K. Polk High

One Day at a Time

A479. Connors and Davenport

A480. Rutledge Toys

A481. Pickles and bananas

A482. PMA Airlines

A483. The Gonigan Travel Agency

A484. The Secret Order of the Beavers

Our Miss Brooks
CBS, 1952–56

Q485. Connie Brooks, a schoolteacher at Madison High School, was in love with shy Philip Boynton, who taught biology. She wished he would take "brave shots" and hoped to one day make a man out of him. Teaching English sometimes tired Connie out and she had invented a means of relaxing after a hard day that she called "School Teachers' B&B." Exactly what was this?

Q486. Philip carried jelly beans with him at all times. "The dextrose contained in them is one of the best sources of quick energy known to science." What color jelly beans was Connie most fond of?

Out of This World
Syndicated, 1987–91

Q487. Thirteen-year-old Evie Garland's mother was an earthling and her father, Troy, an alien from the planet Anterias. It was 1972 when Troy entered Natural Norman's Organic Ice Cream Parlor and saw Donna, a waitress. It was a love at first sight and they married shortly thereafter. What dessert did Troy order?

Q488. Evie attended Marlowe High School and her hangout was a soda shop called the Goodie Goodie. She played third string on the school's basketball team and had a plush cat. What did she call it?

Q489. Although Troy had not seen Evie since she was an infant (when he returned to his planet) he kept in touch with her through a genetic cube. By what term of endearment did Troy call Evie?

Q490. Evie's favorite breakfast was orange juice, hot cakes, and bacon, and her favorite movie star was Kevin Costner. She also loved to wear earrings and had what favorite TV soap opera?

Q491. Before becoming the mayor of Marlowe, California, Donna Garland first ran the Marlowe School for Gifted Children; then a catering service. What was the name of the company?

Our Miss Brooks

A485.   A bed and bath

A486.   The purple ones

Out of This World

A487.   A Raspberry Radish Rocket Ship

A488.   Twinky

A489.   "Earth Angel"

A490.   *All My Yesterday's Tomorrows*

A491.   Donna Delights Planning and Catering

Out of This World continued

Q492. Donna replaced Kyle X. Applegate as mayor when he lost the election by one vote. Kyle was a famous movie and TV star before entering politics, and on television he had three series. *Cowboy Kyle* was one of them; name one of the other two.

Q493. When Kyle was a movie star he portrayed Cowboy Kyle in such films as *The Good, the Bad and the Unattractive* and *Gunfight at the Pretty Good Corral*, which eventually turned into a TV series. Cowboy Kyle wore fancy shirts with ruffles and was assisted by Sheldon Moskowitz, the frontier dentist. Because of his role, Kyle had what off-the-set nickname?

The Patty Duke Show
ABC, 1963–66

Q494. Patty and Cathy Lane were identical cousins living in Brooklyn Heights. Patty was the typical American teenager and Cathy her sophisticated European counterpart. Star Patty Duke also played a third cousin, a blond bombshell version of the two girls who hailed from Atlanta. Patty called her a "Confederate Cleopatra," but what was her real name?

Q495. The Lane family, which also included father Martin, mother Natalie, and brother Ross, lived at 8 Remsen Drive in a house that dated back to the days of George Washington. Who built the place in 1720?

Q496. When Patty thought she could become a teenage sensation as a writer, she wrote a book combining "love, war, poverty, death, and cooking recipes." What did she title it?

Q497. Patty Duke was given the opportunity to sing in several episodes. In one, she acquired a job at the Pink Percolator, a coffeehouse that serves seventy-five different kinds of coffee. Under what name did she work?

A492. *The Floridian* or *Mosquito Man*

A493. "The Ruffleman"

The Patty Duke Show

A494. Betsy Lane

A495. Adam Prescott, whose son, Jonathan, served under Gen. George Washington

A496. *I Was a Teenage Teenager.*

A497. Pittsburgh Patty

The Patty Duke Show continued

Q498. Before coming to America, Cathy lived in Scotland where she attended a private school, where she was the debating champion. What was the name of the school?

Q499. Patty's father, Martin, was the managing editor of the New York *Chronicle* while Cathy's father, Martin's twin, was its foreign correspondent. What paper was in direct competition with the *Chronicle*?

The People's Choice
NBC, 1955–58

Q500. Sock Miller, a councilman in the Fifth District of New City, California, lived in a trailer camp with his Aunt Gus and basset hound Cleo. Before entering politics, Sock was an ornithologist for the Bureau of Fish and Wildlife whose job was to "follow the birds" and file reports on their migratory habits. How many miles had Sock logged following birds?

Q501. When we first met Sock he was tracking down the Yellow-Necked Nuthatch. What was his last assignment before becoming a councilman?

Q502. Sock married Mandy Peoples, the mayor's daughter, in later episodes. What did Mayor Peoples call Sock?

Perfect Strangers
ABC, 1986–93

Q503. Balki Bartokomous hailed from a Mediterranean island called Mypos. Sheepherding was the number one occupation there and the national debt was $635. What animal graced Myposian money?

Q504. When Balki discovered that he had an American cousin (Larry Appleton) living in Chicago, he set out to find him and eventually became his roommate. While Cousin Larry was not of full Myposian blood, how Myposian was he?

A498. Mrs. Tutles of Mountain Briar

A499. The *Record*

The People's Choice

A500. 80,000

A501. To find out why the Rose-breasted Grosbeak was laying smaller eggs this season.

A502. "Nature Boy"

Perfect Strangers

A503. A cow

A504. One sixty-fourth

Perfect Strangers continued

Q505. Balki relished yak links for breakfast and his favorite meal was eel wrapped in grape leaves and sheepherder's bread with a side dish of Ding Ding Mac-Mood (pig snout). He was also a gourmet cook and the best bibibobaca baker on Mypos. What type of dessert was bibibobaca?

Q506. On Mypos, Balki had several pets: a sheep (Dimitri), a three-hundred-pound turtle (Bibby), a horse (Trodsky), and a dog. What did he call the dog?

Q507. Larry was born in May and as a kid had a dog named Spot. His catchphrase was "Oh, My Lord" and he gargled to the tune of what specific song?

Q508. In last-season episodes, Larry married Jennifer and Balki wed her roommate, Mary Anne. The two cousins also become parents. Larry and Jennifer named their son Tucker; what did Balki and Mary Anne name theirs?

The Phil Silvers Show (Sgt. Bilko)
CBS, 1955–59

Q509. The series was originally called *You'll Never Get Rich* and dealt with the moneymaking schemes of endlessly crafty Ernest Bilko, a sergeant with the Company B Motor Pool at Fort Baxter, Kansas. His "career," however, began during World War II, when he was stationed in New Guinea. What was his first scam?

Q510. Bilko moved on to the 24th Division motor pool. What division was he with on New Guinea?

Q511. The base cook, Rupert Ritzik, was Bilko's main patsy. Ritzik read comic books, believed in flying saucers, and was a big fan of TV space shows. What was his favorite series?

A505. Cream puff

A506. Koos Koos

A507. "Moon River"

A508. Robespierre Boinkie

The Phil Silvers Show

A509. Selling USO girls nylons at $5 a pair

A510. The 38th

A511. *Captain Dan, Space Man*

The Powers That Be
NBC, 1992–93

Q512. The Powers were a dysfunctional political family. Bill was a senator; ambitious Margaret, his wife, was yearning to become a First Lady; and their daughter, Caitlin, was married to Theodore, a wimpy congressman. Bill enjoyed Jerry Lewis movies, blueberry muffins, and a martini each night. He had a dog named Little Dickens and loved what one particular song?

Q513. Caitlin had a fear of brunch, allowed only Mr. Sidney to cut her hair, and loved to wear pink. What did she do before each political party?

Q514. Caitlin, who called her mother "Mummy," was pretty, self-serving, and vain. But she also did charity work. What was her favorite charity?

Roc
Fox, 1991–94

Q515. Roc Emerson is a hardworking garbage man with a dream—to own a semidetached house. But until that time comes he lives in an attached house with his wife, Eleanor; his father, Andrew; and his brother, Joey. Roc reads yesterday's news today and has a home furnished mostly with "perks" (items other people discarded that Roc found on his route). It is a hard job, though. How many garbage cans does Roc have to empty to make $2,000?

Q516. Roc's favorite watering hole is Charlene's Bar, but he has coffee with his coworkers at the shop next to the depot. What are either the first or second season names for the coffee shop?

The Powers That Be

A512. "Supercalifragalisticexpialidocious"

A513. Buy a dress one size too small and starve herself until she fit into it.

A514. The Halfway House for Congressmen's Wives

Roc

A515. 175,214

A516. The Dump (first season), then the Landfill

Roseanne
ABC, 1988–

Q517. Roseanne Harris and Dan Conner met in Lanford High School. They dated, married shortly after graduation, set up housekeeping at 714 Delaware Street, and became the parents of three children (Becky, Darlene, and D.J.). Dan's prized possession is his Harley-Davidson motorcycle and he owned a construction company. What did he call it?

Q518. Roseanne held a number of jobs: assembly-line worker, telephone solicitor, order taker, clean-up lady, waitress, and diner owner. She worked the assembly line at Wellman Plastics and was a waitress at Rodbell's Luncheonette. What product did she sell over the phone?

Q519. Sweet and feminine Becky is the oldest child. Her favorite color is red and she enjoys Dannon yogurt. To earn extra money Becky became a cashier at what supermarket?

Q520. Sister Darlene is a tomboy and nasty. She seems to live in her own world and is closer to her father than to her mother. She loves sports and what particular brand of breakfast cereal?

Q521. D.J., the youngest child, has a collection of doll heads and a talent for doing something. Roseanne doesn't know how he manages to do it, but she uses oil to remedy the situation. What "talent" does D.J. have?

Seinfeld
NBC, 1990–

Q522. Events in the daily life of stand-up comedian Jerry Seinfeld can best describe this series. Jerry and his friends Elaine, George, and neighbor across the hall Kramer eat frequently at "The Restaurant," as it is noted in establishing scenes. There is no lettering on the windows in these scenes either. However, an inside shot looking out indicates "The Restaurant" is really what eatery?

Roseanne

A517. 4 Aces Construction

A518. *Discount House* magazine

A519. The Buy 'n' Bag

A520. Fruit Rings

A521. Getting his head stuck in drawers. "He's got a talent for it," says Roseanne.

Seinfeld

A522. Monk's Cafe

Seinfeld continued

Q523. Elaine has the nickname "Nip" around her office after she decided to give a Christmas card of herself to her friends. She didn't realize that her blouse was open at the time and her nipple was showing; neither did the photographer who took the picture. Who snapped the famous "Nip" picture of Elaine?

Q524. When Kramer got the show business bug and thought he could become a great actor, he moved to Hollywood. Although his dream was never realized, Kramer did manage to land a role on *Murphy Brown*. What part did he play?

Silver Spoons
NBC/Syndicated, 1982–88

Q525. Thirty-two-year-old Edward Stratton III was a divorced millionaire who ran the Eddie Toys division of Stratton Industries, a company founded by his great-grandfather, "a banana head who became rich by accident." How did this "banana head" become rich?

Q526. Eddie Toys had its successes and its failures. One of the biggest disasters was a board game that sold six of the fifty thousand units that were produced—and two were returned. What was the game called?

Q527. Now married to Kate, Edward was the father of a twelve-year-old boy named Ricky from his first marriage to Evelyn. Kate was a shoe nut who worried about matching everything with her shoes. When Kate became an active part of Eddie Toys she marketed a Viking doll with an attitude problem. What did she call the doll?

The Simpsons
Fox, 1990–

Q528. The Simpsons are a not-so-typical American cartoon family who live in the small town of Springfield. Homer, the father, is an overweight safety inspector at the local power plant. In what section does he work?

A523. Kramer

A524. "Steve Snell," one of Murphy's parade of secretaries

Silver Spoons

A525. He came up with a rubber inner tube, one year before the invention of the car, as a means of staying afloat in the water when he went to the beach. When Ford made his first car, he used the tube.

A526. Endangered Species

A527. The Viking Warrior

The Simpsons

A528. Sector 7G

The Simpsons continued

Q529. Homer is married to Marge, a thirty-four-year-old blue-beehived housewife and the mother of Bart, Lisa, and Maggie. Bart, TV's bad boy, is the undefeated champ of the video game Slug Fest and his favorite television show is *Krusty the Clown*. He has two pets, a frog and a dog. The dog is called Santa's Little Helper; what did Bart name the frog?

Q530. Practical joke–playing Bart spends much time in the principal's office. He is also a member of the Krusty the Clown fan club and allergic to what specific food?

Q531. Precocious middle child Lisa is a budding saxophone player, reads *Teen Screen* and *Teen Steam* magazines and, while she too watches Krusty the Clown, her favorite TV show is a very violent cartoon. What is it?

Small Wonder
Syndicated, 1985–89

Q532. Short for Voice Input Child Identicate, Vicki was a robot who was created by Ted Lawson as part of a secret experiment to help handicapped children. Ted lived with his wife Joanie and son Jamie in Los Angeles and passed off Vicki (made of plastic, wires, transistors, and micro chips) as his adopted daughter. What invention of Ted's gave Vicki life?

Q533. Vicki had a built-in micro generator and possessed incredible strength. Her brown eyes were solar cells that provide power. What command turned Vicki off?

Q534. Joanie so loved Vicki that she often forgot that the robot was not human. Joanie had dinner ready each night at 6:30 and called leftovers "reruns." "That's nice" was her catchphrase and as a kid she had a pet canary. What did she call it?

A529. Froggie

A530. Butterscotch

A531. *The Itchy and Scratchy Show*

Small Wonder

A532. The Waffer Scale Integration System

A533. Stop

A534. Tweet Tweet

Step by Step
ABC, 1991–

Q535. Carol, a widowed hairdresser with three kids (Dana, Karen and Mark), and Frank, a divorced construction company owner with three kids (Alicia, J.T. and Brendon), marry and attempt to build a new life step by step. They met when Frank came to Carol for a haircut and were married in Jamaica three months later. Where in Jamaica was the ceremony?

Q536. "I'm what the guys call a babe," says fourteen-year-old Karen, often mistaken for a model ("But I'm not"). She is always fashionably dressed and really wants to become a model. Carol believes that her daughter's obsession with herself is her (Carol's) fault because she gave Karen what?

Q537. Fifteen-year-old Dana is Carol's oldest, a straight A student and sensitive to the fact that she has a small bustline. Dana writes for her school newspaper and is the assistant manager of what after-school hangout?

Q538. "You Little Criminal" is one of Dana's "terms of endearment" for Alicia, Frank's pretty twelve-year-old daughter. Alicia is a tomboy, has great potential for the construction business, and had been a member of what all-girl band?

Q539. In 1971 Carol was a contestant in the Miss Small Curd Cottage Cheese Beauty Pageant. She was crowned First Runner-Up. To whom did she lose the title?

Q540. Frank uses a construction site story to explain aspects of the world to the kids. He was president of the Tile and Grout Association and is also a member of what lodge?

Taxi
ABC/NBC, 1978–83

Q541. Louie DePalma was the nasty, snide dispatcher for the Sunshine Cab Company in Manhattan. His office was called the Cage and he believed all his drivers to be losers. According to Louie, only one cabbie made it out and so far had not returned. Who was it?

Step by Step

A535.   The Wedding Shack

A536.   A Brooke Shields doll

A537.   The '50s Cafe

A538.   Chicks with Attitudes

A539.   "I lost to a girl with bigger curds."

A540.   The Mallard Lodge

Taxi

A541.   James Caan—"But he'll be back. They all come back."

Taxi *continued*

Q542. Louie lived for his job at the company and had been there fifteen years, first as a driver, then as the dispatcher. He liked bookings high and would appreciate a call if a cabbie cannot make his shift. But he hated what one word, a word he didn't want to hear ("Never, never say the word!")?

Q543. Lecherous, money-worshipping Louie considered himself a ladies' man even though cabbie Alex Reiger remarked, "If God had a reason for creating snakes, lice, and vermin, He had a reason for creating Louie." Lady cabbie Elaine Nardo was often the unencouraged object of Louie's lust. What did he call her breasts?

Q544. Cabbie Bobby Wheeler, an aspiring actor who starred in a one-man play called *Charles Darwin Tonight*, also played the role of Skip on what TV soap opera?

Q545. James Caldwell, a once brilliant Harvard student who became somewhat spaced-out on drugs and believed he is living in the 1960s, changed his name to Jim Ignatowski when he believed "Star Child" was Ignatowski spelled backward. In 1968 he was ordained as Reverend Jim. In what Church was he a minister?

That Girl
ABC, 1966–71

Q546. "That Girl" was Ann Marie, a small-towner who came to the big city to further her career as an actress. Earlier she had won a medal as Best Actress at Camp Winnepoo and was a member of her college drama club. While not having the greatest qualifications, she was still accepted into what drama school?

Q547. Acting jobs were not always easy to come by and Ann took any one she could find to help pay the bills. She worked as a model, door-to-door shoe salesgirl, and a spokesgirl for a fast food chicken product. What was she?

Q548. Ann's TV debut was on an unnamed show playing a bank teller. Her most embarrassing moment also happened on television. What was it?

A542. Accident

A543. Headlights

A544. *For Better, For Worse*

A545. The Church of the Peaceful

That Girl

A546. The Benedict Workshop of the Dramatic Arts

A547. "Miss Chicken Big" for Chicken Big, Inc.

A548. She played a corpse and opened her eyes on camera on live TV.

That Girl continued

Q549. Lou Marie, Ann's father, disapproved of her career until he let her direct his local stage group at the Brewster Country Club. Lou had become famous in Brewster for his rendition of what vaudeville song?

Three's Company
ABC, 1977–84

Q550. Janet Wood, Chrissy Snow, and Jack Tripper shared Apartment 201 at the Ropers' Apartment House in California. Janet was a store manager, Chrissy worked as a secretary, and Jack was a cooking student who pretended to be gay to live in the apartment and was studying French cuisine. ("You're looking at the Galloping Gourmet of 1980"). What cooking school was he attending?

Q551. Janet was born in Massachusetts and had a tendency to nag a lot. She was first a salesgirl, then the manager of what store?

Q552. Sexy Chrissy Snow was born on December 25. She was very sweet and trusting and her real name was Christmas Snow. To supplement her income as a secretary, she took a second job selling cosmetics. What was the name of the products?

The Tony Randall Show
ABC/CBS, 1976–78

Q553. Walter Oliver Franklin was a widower and the father of two children, Roberta and Oliver, Jr. Walter was born on June 17 and lived in Philadelphia. He was a less-than-magisterial judge with what court system?

Q554. To earn extra money, Walter took a job teaching law at a less-than-prestigious school. Name it.

A549.   "Minnie the Moocher"

Three's Company

A550.   The L.A. Technical School

A551.   The Arcade Florist Shop

A552.   Easy Time Cosmetics

The Tony Randall Show

A553.   The Court of Common Pleas

A554.   Ed's School of Law

Too Close for Comfort
ABC/Syndicated, 1980–86

Q555. Henry Rush, wife, Muriel, and grown daughters, Jackie and Sarah, lived in a red Victorian house in San Francisco. Henry was a cartoonist and creator of the comic book "Cosmic Cow," a space crime fighter. What was his biggest challenge when sketching Cosmic Cow?

Q556. In order to keep tabs on Jackie and Sarah, Henry rented them the downstairs apartment for how much a month?

Q557. Sarah, a college student, took various part-time jobs to pay her half of the rent. She got her first job as a "wench waitress" because she had a figure that fit the available costume. What was the bar called?

Q558. Henry's daily aggravation stemmed not only from keeping tabs on Jackie and Sarah, but also from his tenant, Monroe Ficus, a lost soul who sort of attached himself to Sarah. Monroe worked as a security guard and was once named Officer April for catching a shoplifter. Where did Monroe work?

227
NBC, 1985–90

Q559. Housewife Mary Jenkins was president of the tenant's association of an apartment house at 227 in Washington. Her husband, Lester, was an engineer with the Stumer and Nathan Construction Company. Where did Mary work?

Q560. To supplement her weekly allowance, daughter Brenda became a burger bagger at what fast food store?

Q561. Of all the residents at 227, the most colorful was beautiful Sandra Clark, who knew she was a threat to other men's wives and used her wiles to get men to do what she wanted. Sandra had a favorite letter of the alphabet. What is it?

Q562. Sandra came to 227 as a college student. She was a bombshell then and had a nickname. What was it?

Too Close for Comfort

A555.   "To draw an udder so it is not offensive."

A556. $300

A557.   The Fox and Hound

A558.   Riverwood Shopping Mall

227

A559.   Winslow Travel Agency

A560.   Billy Bob's Burger Barge

A561.   "M—for money, men, and me."

A562.   "Sparkles"

Webster
ABC/Syndicated, 1983–88

Q563. Seven-year-old Webster Long resided with his godfather, George Papadopolis, and George's wife, Katherine. Webster kept his "menstoes" (mementos) in an old cigar box and he had a teddy bear, two frogs, a snake, and a home-made robot. He called the teddy bear Teddy, but what was his name for the robot?

Q564. Webster ate Sugar Sweeties cereal for breakfast, played trumpet in the school band, and enjoyed feeding the pigeons in the park. He had named a number of them but had a favorite. Which one was it?

Welcome Back, Kotter
ABC, 1975–79

Q565. Gabe Kotter was a graduate of James Buchanan High School who returned ten years later to teach Special Guidance Remedial Academics to a class of delinquents known as Sweathogs (Vinnie Barbarino, Juan Epstein, Freddy Washington, and Arnold Horshack). Before becoming a teacher, Gabe had aspired to become a comedian. Where did he perform his stand-up routines?

Q566. There were three Mary Johnsons at Buchanan High. The plain and sensitive Mary Johnson was Arnold's girlfriend. What were the other two Mary Johnsons called?

Q567. While the Sweathogs were hardly students, they were street smart and knew how to handle themselves on the sidewalks of Brooklyn. When they pooled their resources to buy a car, what did they call it?

Webster

A563. Mr. Spielberg

A564. Charlie

Welcome Back, Kotter

A565. The Comedy Connection Club

A566. Mary the cheerleader; Mary the athlete

A567. The Sweatmobile

What's Happening!!
ABC, 1976–79

Q568. Raj, Dwayne, and Rerun were three friends who lived in Southern California and attended Jefferson High School. Raj had ambitions to become a writer and was editor of the school newspaper, the *Gazette*. "Mr. Beaver Builds a Dam and Saves the Town of Gum Drop Falls" was the title of the first story Raj wrote. What magazine published it?

Q569. Rerun's real name was Freddie Stubbs. His nickname came from his habit of repeating in summer school what he should have learned in the fall. Before becoming a page at KABC-TV, Rerun was a member of what rock group?

Who's the Boss?
ABC, 1984–92

Q570. Tony Micelli, a widower and the father of a young girl, Samantha, worked as the housekeeper to Angela Bower, a high-powered ad exec and divorcée with a young son, Jonathan. Before a career-ending injury, Tony was a professional ball player and was second baseman for two seasons. For what team did Tony play?

Q571. Samantha was affectionately called Sam. French toast was her favorite breakfast and she called it "Mr. Frenchie." Pasta, which she referred to as "Mr. Linguini," was her favorite dinner. She also had a favorite plush teddy bear. What was her name for it?

Q572. Before beginning her own ad company, the Angela Bower Agency, Angela was the president of another agency in Manhattan. Name the one she headed.

Q573. As a teenager, Angela attended the Montague Academy for Girls. While not as popular as she would have liked to be (she called herself a geek because she was not as busty as the other girls), she did manage to find some happiness as a member of what singing group?

What's Happening!!

A568. *Little Miss Muffet*

A569. The Rockets

Who's the Boss?

A570. St. Louis Cardinals

A571. Freddy Fuzzy Face

A572. Wallace and McQuade

A573. The Curlets

Who's the Boss? continued

Q574. Mona, Angela's ultrasexy mother and her assistant at the ad agency, was rather well developed and constantly reminded her daughter that she lacks cleavage. What was the "term of endearment" Mona's mother had for her?

WKRP in Cincinnati
CBS, 1978–82

Q575. WKRP was a 5,000 watt AM radio station located on the ninth floor of the Flem Building. The highest rating it ever achieved was number 14 and the "Big Guy," Arthur Carlson, ran the station for his overbearing mother. Blond bombshell Jennifer Marlowe, the highest paid employee at the station, worked as the receptionist. How much a year did she make?

Q576. Jennifer, described by other women as "the best-looking woman I have ever seen," would only date older men (she feels safer with them) and lived in a gorgeous apartment with a unique doorbell. When rung, what song did it play?

Q577. The station couldn't afford a news van so Les Nessman, the station's lovably nerdy news director, used his motor scooter as the WKRP mobile news unit. Les was very proud of his news broadcasts, especially the hog reports segment. What award had Les won for these reports?

Q578. Venus Flytrap was the late night disc jockey. His real name was Gordon Sims, but he was in hiding and changed his named after going AWOL. How long was Gordon in the army before he deserted?

Q579. WKRP's 1978 Thanksgiving episode was perhaps the most famous one of any series, in which Arthur devised a plan to wish his listeners a happy holiday and hired a helicopter with a banner that read "Happy Thanksgiving." Passing over a mall, he dropped live turkeys from two thousand feet. Shoppers begin running for their lives as the turkeys hit the ground like wet bags of cement. "As God is my witness," Arthur said, "I thought turkeys could fly." What was the name of the mall that was bombarded with turkeys?

A574. "All boobs and no brains."

WKRP in Cincinnati

A575. $24,000

A576. "Fly Me to the Moon"

A577. The Silver Sow Award

A578. Ten months and 29 days

A579. The Pine Dale Shopping Mall

CHAPTER
2
Drama and Adventure

The A-Team
NBC, 1983–87

Q580. Hannibal Smith, B.A. Baracus, H.M. Murdock, and Templeton Peck were the A-Team, Vietnam buddies wanted by the army, who helped people in trouble. What military leader framed the A-Team for robbing the bank of Hanoi?

Q581. B.A. stood for Bad Attitude and he lived up to that name although he was a pussycat around children. What was the nickname his mother gave him?

Q582. Murdock lived in the psychiatric ward of the VA Hospital in Los Angeles and was believed to be suffering from paranoid delusions. What key word triggered his aggression?

Q583. Although Murdock and B.A. appeared to have nothing in common and B.A. honestly believed Murdock to be crazy, they did share one thing—the same blood type. What type was it?

Q584. Murdock had two heroes, one from an old TV show, the other the spokesman for a hamburger food chain. Name either one of them.

Q585. Templeton, nicknamed "Face," was raised in an orphanage and learned most of his cons by watching TV. He used that knowledge to scrounge for the team what they needed. What TV series was so helpful to Face?

The A-Team

A580.   Col. Samuel Morrison

A581.   "Scooter"

A582.   Ammonia

A583.   A-B Negative

A584   *The Range Rider* or Captain Bellybuster of Burger Heaven

A585.   *Dragnet*

Adventures in Paradise
ABC, 1959–62

Q586. Adam Troy was a Korean War veteran who owned a schooner named the *Tiki* and earned a living by ferrying passengers and cargo in Tahiti. The schooner had a temperamental engine. What did Troy call the engine?

Q587. While Adam did set sail for exotic adventures, he had a home base on Tahiti. Where did he anchor the *Tiki* and what was his address?

Q588 In last-season episodes, Clay Baker jumped ship to become the owner of a hotel He also made a reputation for himself as a bartender. Name the two drinks for which he was famous.

Airwolf
CBS, 1984–86

Q589. Airwolf was an awesome attack helicopter piloted by Stringfellow Hawke. To protect the chopper from the government officials who wanted it back, Hawke had hidden it in a secluded area in California. What did he call Airwolf's hiding place?

Q590. Hawke liked privacy and lived in a remote section of California with a dog. Name his companion.

Q591. Airwolf was built by the U.S. Government, then stolen and held hostage by Hawke until his brother, listed as missing in Vietnam, was located. What was Airwolf's file number?

Q592. Airwolf was a Bell 222 helicopter and equipped with computers, missiles, and chain guns in its wings. What was its cruising speed?

Q593. Hawke's partner, Dominic Santini, ran his own air charter service from the Municipal Airport in California. On what island was Dom born?

Adventures in Paradise

A586. "The Lady"

A587. The *Tiki* is anchored at the Papeete Harbor; Troy's address is the Schooner *Tiki*.

A588. Tahitian Madness and the Polynesian Rainmaker

Airwolf

A589. Valley of the Gods

A590. Tet

A591. A56-7W

A592. 300 knots

A593. San Remo

The Avengers
ABC, 1966–69

Q594. Debonair British agent John Steed exuded Old World charm, drove a vintage Bentley, and took his coffee with three sugars. He also had an Achilles' heel. What was it?

Q595. The sexy, totally emancipated Emma Peel partnered with Steed for the sheer love of adventure. Emma never worked; she inherited what company from her late father?

Q596. "Better Bridge Through Applied Mathematics" was the famous article Emma wrote for the June issue of what magazine?

Q597. Before Steed was teamed with the shapely Tara King, Emma Peel's replacement, he "met" her when she accidentally tackled him during a training exercise assignment. What was Tara's agent recruiting number?

Banacek
NBC, 1972–74

Q598. Thomas Banacek, a free-lance, Boston-based insurance investigator who recovered lost or stolen objects, also operated his own business. What was it?

Q599. For his research, Banacek used the Recovery and Rewards section of what paper?

Q600. Carlie Kirkland, Banacek's competitor, worked in what department of the Boston Insurance Company?

Batman
ABC, 1966–68

Q601. Millionaire Bruce Wayne and his youthful ward, Dick Grayson, lived at stately Wayne Manor with Alfred, their ever-faithful butler. Batman and Robin never mixed crimefighting with eating; however, after each assignment, they were treated to what meal by Alfred?

The Avengers

A594.   The opposite sex

A595.   Knight Industries

A596.   *The Bridge Players International Guide*

A597.   Agent 69

Banacek

A598.   T. Banacek—Restorations

A599.   *The Assurance Reports*

A600.   Property and Recovery Division

Batman

A601.   Milk and sandwiches

Batman continued

Q602. While Batman did have a fun side (for example, he invented a dance called the Batusi), he could not abide one thing. What was it?

Q603. Assisting Batman and Robin was Barbara Gordon, alias Batgirl. While Barbara worked for the Gotham City library, she was also chairperson of what Gotham City committee?

Q604. Alfred was the only one to know the true identities of Batman and Robin. He also assisted them in the field. When the phone rang at Wayne Manor, what were the words Alfred used to answer it?

Q605. Barbara lived in midtown Gotham City in Apartment 8A with her pet bird. What was its name?

Q606. As Batgirl, Barbara received the first Gotham City Female Crime Fighting and Fashion Award. What was the award called?

Baywatch
NBC/Syndicated, 1989–

Q607. Mitch Buchannan originally shared outpost tower 27 with Jill Riley. While attempting to save swimmers from a shark sighting, Jill, a lifeguard with Baywatch, was attacked by the animals and suffered massive internal injuries. She never recovered and mentioned that she never had the opportunity to finish reading what book that she began as a teenager?

Q608. After breaking up with her husband, Mitch, Gayle left California for a job in another state. At what fast food place did she find employment?

Q609. Lifeguard Shauni McClain attended South Central High School and received $50 from her parents for every A on her report card. Shauni uses a specific brand of sun block when working on the beach. Name it.

A602. Being called a coward

A603. The Anti-Littering Committee

A604. "Stately Wayne Manor"

A605. Charlie

A606. The Battie

Baywatch

A607. *Wuthering Heights*

A608. Captain Cluck's Chicken and Fixin' Franchises

A609. "Bohemian Love"

Baywatch *continued*

Q610. Summer Quinn is a beautiful lifeguard trainee who replaced Shauni in 1992. What was Summer's greatest fear during training?

Beauty and the Beast
CBS, 1987–90

Q611. The subterranean world beneath the New York subway system was home to Vincent, the beast, and Father, the leader of a group of misfit people. In this world without telephones, TV's or radios, how did the people keep in contact with one another?

Q612. The tunnels where this underground society lived led to all areas of the city, giving them access to the outside world. Which part of this subterranean community was most dangerous for these people?

Q613. The people of the underworld had contacts in the world above who kept their secret and assisted them. What were these people called?

Q614. In the final episode, Vincent (the beast of the title), had a son by Catherine Chandler (beauty). What did Vincent name his son?

Beverly Hills, 90210
Fox, 1990–

Q615. Brenda and Brandon Walsh are sixteen-year-old fraternal twins who now attend West Beverly Hills High. Brenda is the older twin; by how much?

Q616. Brenda's favorite TV show is *Keep It Together*, but it was Brandon who landed a role on it. When Brenda had to substitute for Brandon at the Peach Pit as a waitress, what name did she use?

Q617. When the family lived in Minnesota, Brenda and Brandon were both straight A students. Brenda was a member of the drama club and Brandon wrote for the school newspaper. What was Brandon called at school?

A610. Diving off the 100-foot pier

Beauty and the Beast

A611. Tapping on the underground pipes that run throughout the city

A612. Prince Street on Manhattan's lower East Side

A613. Helpers

A614. Jacob

Beverly Hills, 90210

A615. Four minutes

A616. Laverne

A617. Mr. Popularity

Beverly Hills, 90210 continued

Q618. As a kid Brenda had two plush toys—a horse and a lion. She called the lion "Mr. Lion." What did she call the horse?

Q619. Jim, Brenda and Brandon's father, calls Brandon "Big Guy." What does he call Brenda?

The Bionic Woman
ABC/NBC, 1976–78

Q620. "The Home of American Astronaut Steve Austin" was the sign one saw on entering this small town in California where Jaime Sommers, the Bionic Woman of the title, also lived. Name the town.

Q621. Days before her almost fatal skydiving accident, tennis pro Jaime Sommers was scheduled to play what opponent in Spain?

Q622. Rudy Wells, the bionic surgeon responsible for Jaime's upkeep, invented a taffy-like substance that could, in essence, give anybody bionic powers. The substance was deadly, however, if taken in large doses. What did Dr. Wells call his discovery?

Q623. In addition to the role of Jaime Sommers, Lindsay Wagner played a girl who, through plastic surgery, became a Jaime Sommers lookalike. This Jaime, however, was up to no good, and sought the secret of the real Jaime's powers. What was her name?

B.J. and the Bear
NBC, 1979–81

Q624. B.J. McKay was a trucker who traveled with his simian companion, Bear, across the country. B.J. would haul anything legal anywhere for how much a mile?

Q625. B.J. was a POW in Vietnam when he found Bear (Bear would bring him food to help him survive). After whom did B.J. name Bear?

A618. Mr. Pony

A619. "Beautiful"

The Bionic Woman

A620. Ojai

A621. Billie Jean King

A622. Hydrazene

A623. Lisa Galloway

B.J. and the Bear

A624. $1.50

A625. After Paul "Bear" Bryant, whom B.J. considered to be a great football coach

B.J. and the Bear continued

Q626. B.J. also had another name for Bear and he often called him by this. What was it?

Q627. B.J. played the sax and he once did so with a band. Name the band.

Q628. When B.J. set up his own business (Bear Enterprises) he did so over a bar where two of his truckers, twins Geri and Teri, worked. What was the name of the bar?

Q629. One of B.J.'s seven lady truckers (last-season episodes) had a crush on him, but exclaimed "B.J. sees me only as a girl who can drive a rig and fix a flat tire." Not as feminine as the other girls, she also had what B.J. calls "a smart mouth." Who was she?

Bourbon Street Beat
ABC, 1959–60

Q630. The detective firm of Randolph and Calhoun was located on Bourbon Street in the French Quarter of New Orleans. Name the famous nightclub located next to it.

Q631. Rex Randolph, the senior partner, was an Ivy League man and loved to cook. Before becoming Rex's partner, Cal Calhoun was a lieutenant with what police department?

Q632. The firm's receptionist, Melody Lee Mercer, yearned to become a detective. She was born in Louisiana and won a 1958 beauty pageant. What title was it?

Q633. Kenny Madison was a part-time detective who works for Rex. He was studying to become a lawyer and attended what university?

Buck Rogers in the 25th Century
NBC, 1979–81

Q634. After drifting in space for almost five hundred years, Buck's rocket, the Ranger III, was found by Princess Ardella, the commander of a two-mile-wide space craft. What was the name of her ship?

A626. "The Kid"

A627. Ghettoway City

A628. Phil's Disco

A629. Callie

Bourbon Street Beat

A630. The Old Absinthe House

A631. Pelican Point P.D.

A632. Miss U.S.A. in the 1958 Miss Universe Pageant

A633. Tulane

Buck Rogers in the 25th Century

A634. The King's Flagship Draconia

Buck Rogers in the 25th Century *continued*

Q635. Finding that he could not go back to his time, Buck joined Wilma Deering and Dr. Elias Huer to help with their future. What did Buck become a member of?

Q636. In this future world the retirement age had risen to eighty-five and America had a new capital. What was it?

Charlie's Angels
ABC, 1976–81

Q637. Sabrina Duncan, Jill Munroe, and Kelly Garrett were the original "Charlie's Angels." Each was a former officer with the L.A.P.D. Jill's sister, Kris Munroe, replaced her; Tiffany Welles replaced Sabrina; and Julie Rogers replaced Tiffany. Julie was also an L.A.P.D. officer, but what police departments did Tiffany and Kris represent?

Q638. The angels never saw their employer. Charlie contacted them via a telephone (usually heard over a speaker phone) or through his representative, John Bosley. What company did Charlies own that required the services of three angels?

China Beach
ABC, 1988–91

Q639. The U.S. Armed Forces R&R facility in Danang was the 510 Evac Hospital, 63rd Division. The unit was unable to handle critical neurological surgery, but took care of virtually everything else. How many beds and how many surgical units were there?

Q640. Colleen McMurphy was a triage nurse who volunteered for service in Vietnam. What was she called when she first arrived on China Beach?

Q641. Colleen desperately wanted to do her job while at the same time overcome her feelings of frustration. In all the time she spent on China Beach, she had only one wish. What was it?

A635.   The Third Force of the Earth Directorate

A636.   New Chicago

Charlie's Angels

A637.   Tiffany (Boston), Kris (San Francisco)

A638.   Townsend Investigations or the Townsend Detective Agency

China Beach

A639.   180 beds, 33 surgical units

A640.   F.N.G. (Fairly New Guy)

A641.   A day without choppers (which brought the wounded)

China Beach continued

Q642. K.C. was the only civilian on China Beach. She was a high-priced prostitute and charged how much an hour?

Q643. K.C. was from Kansas City, but the K.C. stood for something else—K.C.'s real name. What was it?

Q644. Colleen and Karen first saw each other in the women's shower. K.C. noticed Colleen staring at her navel and said what to her?

Q645. Something made K.C. feel safe as a child; she would snuggle under the bed covers and gain a sense of safety. On China Beach this same thing provided her with the only sense of safety she could feel amid the devastation that surrounded her. What was it?

Q646. Boonewell "Boonie" Lanier was with the First Marine Division, Icor, on China Beach. What did he always call K.C.?

Q647. Laurette Barber was a single-dancer with the USO touring Vietnam. Although it was not part of her job, she helped Colleen in times of emergency. Laurette never had a family and grew up in what orphanage?

Q648. In one of the most emotional episodes of any series, Cherry White, the sweet Red Cross nurse who volunteered for duty in Nam, was killed in a bombing before she could accomplish her greatest desire. What was it?

CHiPs
NBC, 1977–83

Q649. Ponch Poncherello and Jon Baker were members of CHiPs, the California Highway Patrol. What brand of motorcycle did the officers ride?

Q650. Officer Bonnie Clark took sign communication at Cal State and was now a part of the Deaf Liaison Program. What nickname did Ponch have for her?

A642. $100.

A643. Karen Colosky

A644. "Never seen an outie before?"

A645. The rain

A646. "K.C. from K.C."

A647. Lady of Perpetual Hope

A648. To find her brother Rick, who was reported as missing in action

CHiPs

A649. Kawasaki

A650. "Bon Bon"

CHiPs continued

Q65I. The police department attempted to introduce efficiency in CHiPs via a robotics program. What was the program called?

Civil Wars
ABC, 1991–93

Q652. Sydney Guilford, Charlie Howell, and Eli Levinson were three friends who operated a law firm in New York City that handled divorces. What was their retainer and what was their hourly rate?

Q653. Denise Ianello, the firm's pretty but sometimes far-out legal secretary, was born in New York, went to P.S. 147 grammar school, and Sacred Heart High School. What secretarial school did she attend?

Columbo
NBC/ABC, 1971–91

Q654. Lieutenant Columbo is famous for his rumpled raincoat and pretense of muddleheadedness. He felt there was something wrong with him "because I seem to bother people and make them nervous." The viewer knew Columbo was closing in on a culprit when he uttered his famous catchphrase. What is it?

Q655. Columbo enjoyed his coffee hot, strong, and black, drove a battered Peugeot, and had two dogs. The first one (when the series was on NBC) was Fang. When the series switched to ABC (1989–91) what did Columbo call the dog?

Q656. Columbo smoked cigars but his never-seen wife preferred pipes if he must smoke. Why wouldn't Columbo smoke a pipe?

A651.   MERV (Maximum Efficiency Robotization, Vector Section 1)

Civil Wars

A652. $7,500 retainer; $300 an hour

A653.   The Kathie Gibbs School

Columbo

A654.   "Oh, one more thing."

A655.   "Dog. He's a dog so we call him dog."

A656.   "It's too much for me to carry around."

The Commish
ABC, 1990–95

Q657. Tony Scali, the chief of the Eastbridge Police Department, is affectionately called "The Commish." He was born in Brooklyn and attended St. Mary's High School. From what real college did Tony get his law degree?

Q658. Tony dreams of becoming the police commissioner and is studying to do just that. In the opening theme Tony is seen reading a book. What book is it?

Q659. Tony's loving wife, Rachel, is a teacher—at what school?

Dark Shadows
ABC, 1966–71

Q660. Victoria Winters was a young woman who came to the fishing village of Collinsport to become the tutor to nine-year-old David Collins, who lived with his father, Roger; Roger's sister, Elizabeth; and Elizabeth's daughter, Carolyn. The family owned the town and resided in what mansion on the Collinswood Estates?

Q661. Victoria soon discovered the supernatural to be present on the estate. She was helped at times by the spirit of Josette Collins, who killed herself a century earlier by jumping off a forbidding cliff overlooking the ocean. What was this area called?

Q662. When Josette appeared, there was no mistaking her presence. Her portrait glowed and the scent of her perfume was evident. What scent was it?

Q663. Barnabas Collins was a 175-year-old vampire who was set free by Willie Loomis when seeking the jewels that were supposedly buried with Barnabas. Barnabas was concealed in a secret room in the family crypt. Where is the crypt located?

The Commish

A657.   Fordham University in the Bronx

A658.   *Tissue Decomposition: A Homicide Primer*

A659.   The Eastbridge Grammar School

Dark Shadows

A660.   The Great House

A661.   Widow's Hill

A662.   Jasmine

A663.   Eagle Hill Cemetery

Doogie Howser, M.D.
ABC, 1989–93

Q664. Sixteen-year-old Doogie Howser was not a normal teenager; he was a genius and a doctor with the Eastman Medical Center. When Doogie wanted to see if he could become just another teen, he took a part-time job at what fast-food emporium?

Q665. Doogie's friend, Vinnie, was a budding film director hoping to get into California's Institute of the Arts. In an attempt to impress a producer, Vinnie wrote a movie script called what?

Q666. At the end of each episode Doogie was seen entering the day's activities into his computer. What did he call these notes?

The Dukes of Hazzard
CBS, 1979–85

Q667. Jefferson Davis Hogg, the corrupt "Boss" of rural Hazzard County, Georgia, attempted to control the town but was continually foiled by the Dukes, a peace-loving clan who felt it was their duty to right wrongs. Uncle Jesse was the head of the family and he ran a farm with nephews Bo and Luke and niece Daisy. What was the location of the Duke farm?

Q668. "The law is the law and we Dukes gotta obey it no matter what," says Uncle Jesse. But at one point Jesse was a lawbreaker. What did he do?

Q669. Bo and Luke had a souped-up 1969 Dodge Charger called the General Lee. The car had the racing number 1 on its sides. What was on the roof?

Q670. Daisy's mode of transportation was not as fancy as Bo or Luke's: she drove a jeep. What did she call it?

Q671. Sheriff Roscoe P. Coltrane was Boss Hogg's corrupt assistant. He had office number 101 and patrolled the streets with his bloodhound. What was the dog's name?

Doogie Howser, M.D.

A664. Burger Baby

A665. *The Black Lizard*

A666. "The Personal Journal of Doogie Howser, M.D."

The Dukes of Hazzard

A667. Old Mill Road

A668. Ran moonshine from his stills

A669. The Confederate flag

A670. Dixie

A671. Flash

Dynasty
ABC, 1981–89

Wealthy Blake Carrington was married to Krystle. He owned a mansion at 173 Essex Drive in Denver, Colorado, and ran the Denver-Carrington Oil Company Name the businesses of these other *Dynasty* regulars:

Q672. Alexis Carrington Colby, Blake's ex-wife, owns what oil company?

Q673. Blake's daughter, Fallon, runs what hotel?

Q674. Sammy Jo Dean, Krystle's niece, operates what stables?

Q675. The woman of mystery, Dominque Devereaux, owns what record company?

Eight Is Enough
ABC, 1977–81

Q676. The Bradfords were a ten-member family who lived in Sacramento. Tom was married to Abby, his second wife, but had eight children by his first wife, Joanie. David, the oldest son, was a contractor and formed the Bradford Construction Company with Tom. For what company did David work before starting his own business?

Q677. Family friend Dr. Craig Maxwell was oldest daughter Mary Bradford's inspiration to become a doctor. At what hospital did Mary intern?

Q678. Joanie was named after her mother and had her mother's eyes, smile, and sensitivity. She was first a researcher, then a reporter, for what TV station?

Q679. Nancy was the prettiest of the Bradford girls. Before acquiring a job at a brokerage house, Nancy worked as a model in TV commercials. What product did she represent?

Q680. Susan, the most sensitive of the girls and the most indecisive about her future, eventually found her calling operating a day care center. She was also the second child to wed (David was first), marrying Merle Stockwell, a ballplayer for what team?

Dynasty

A672. Colbyco

A673. LaMirage

A674. Delta Rho

A675. Titiana

Eight Is Enough

A676. Mann Construction

A677. St. Mary's

A678. KTNS, Channel 8

A679. She was the Sunshine Soda Girl.

A680. The Cyclones

Eight Is Enough *continued*

Q681. Tommy was the most troublesome of the Bradford children. He was rebellious and wanted to quit school to become a rock musician. Name the band he started.

Q682. Elizabeth and Nicholas were the youngest kids. Elizabeth had aspirations to become a dancer. Nicholas was in grammar school and had two pet hamsters. What were their names?

The Fall Guy
ABC, 1981–86

Q683. "I'm not the kind to kiss and tell but I've been seen with Farrah...I've gotten burned over Cheryl Tiegs, blown up for Raquel Welch...I'm the unknown stuntman who makes Eastwood look so fine..." So said the theme as it described Colt Seavers, a movie and TV stuntman for what organization?

Q684. Colt was also a bounty hunter for the Los Angeles Criminal Courts System. He worked for several different bailbondsmen, but what did he carry as a weapon "to impress people"?

Q685. Living in a cabin in the woods that was somewhat off the beaten path, Colt found that soaking in his outdoor tub relaxed him. He also had a favorite watering hole. What was it?

Q686. Samantha Jack, Teri Michaels, and Pearl Sperling were the bailbonds"men" who hired Colt to track down criminals. What company did the women represent?

Q687. Colt's cousin, Howie Munson, was a budding stuntman who worked as Colt's business manager. What did Colt call Howie?

A681. Tommy and the Actions

A682. Ron and Marsha

The Fall Guy

A683. Fall Guy Stunt Association

A684. A movie stuntgun with three-quarter-load blanks

A685. The Palomino Club

A686. Bond Street Bail

A687. "Kid"

Family
ABC, 1976–80

Q688. The Lawrences were a middle-income family of six living in Pasadena. Doug, a lawyer, and his wife, Kate, were the parents of Nancy, Willie, Buddy and Annie. At the start of the second season Quinn Cummings joined the cast as Annie Cooper, an eleven-year-old who came to live with the Lawrences when her parents were killed in a car accident. What were her parents' first names?

Q689. Doug and Kate's oldest, Nancy, was attending law school, while middle child Willie worked for a TV game show that was a takeoff on *The Dating Game*. What was it called?

Q690. Buddy, whose real name is Letitia, was the "baby" of the family. She and Annie attended the same school. Name it.

Fantasy Island
ABC, 1978–84

Q691. "Da plane, da plane." These words, spoken by diminutive Tattoo, indicated that guests were arriving on Fantasy Island to have their dreams granted by Mr. Roarke, the mysterious owner of the place. Mr. Roarke appeared to be an immortal (he was over three hundred years old) and for centuries had been battling what evil?

Q692. Fantasy Island was, of course, totally surrounded by water, in which lived many strange creatures. It was known, for example, that a mermaid called these waters home. Michelle Phillips played the role. What was her name?

Family

A688. Grace and Ralph

A689. *The Dame Game*

A690. Quenton Junior High

Fantasy Island

A691. The Devil

A692. Princess Nyah

Father Dowling Mysteries
NBC/ABC, 1989–91

Q693. Father Dowling and Sister Steve, a novice nun, were amateur detectives who helped the police solve crimes. Father Dowling had been pastor at St. Michael's parish for nine years and was a Chicago Cubs fan. Sherlock Holmes was his hero and he was an avid mystery book and magazine reader. What is his favorite magazine?

Q694. Father Dowling first met Stevie at F.W. Woolworth. She was a juvie and he caught her shoplifting. Under his guidance her life was turned around. When she received her confirmation, Stevie took an unusual middle name. What was it?

Q695. Sister Steve loved to visit the zoo. When she was a kid she befriended a monkey that to this day looked forward to seeing her. What did she name the monkey?

Q696. When a TV producer read of Father Dowling's exploits in the local newspaper, he came to Chicago to make a series based on the priest's adventures. What was the series to be called?

The Flash
CBS, 1990–91

Q697. Before Barry Allen became the Flash, a crimefighter in Central City in 1990, there had been another champion of the underdog. He rode in a black car, wore a black costume, and used "Tranq bullets." Who was he?

Q698. Barry Allen turned into the Flash when he was accidentally dowsed with chemicals. His assistant was Tina McGee, a government scientist who helped him establish his Flash alias. For what agency did Tina work?

Q699. The Flash was capable of fantastic speeds and required much food to maintain his strength. Tina had calculated how fast Barry could run; in fact he could cause sonic booms. Just what was Barry's speed?

Father Dowling Mysteries

A693. *Armchair Sleuth*

A694. Sivle (Elvis spelled backwards)

A695. Diogenes

A696. *Father Flaherty Investigates*

The Flash

A697. The Night Shade

A698. Star Labs

A699. 620 mph

Fly by Night
CBS, 1990–92

Q700. Slick Air was a one-plane airline owned by Sally Monroe that could handle thirty passengers. What kind of plane did Sally own?

Q701. The Federal Trade Development Bank held the mortgage on Slick Air. Sally's business was based at the Ellis Airport and she lived nearby in Vancouver. What was Sally's favorite watering hole?

The Greatest American Hero
ABC, 1981–83

Q702. To prevent Earth from destroying itself, aliens from an unknown planet chose two earthlings to wage a war on crime: Ralph Hinkley, a schoolteacher, and Bill Maxwell, an FBI agent. The aliens selected Ralph to become the Greatest American Hero because he possessed three qualities. Name them.

Q703. The aliens gave Ralph a costume that endowed him with special powers. Ralph called it "the suit." What was Bill's name for it?

Q704. While Ralph did try to keep his newfound abilities a secret, many people witnessed his amazing feats. What newspaper was first to publish a picture of Ralph flying?

Q705. Bill referred to the aliens as "the little green guys" and sometimes has a difficult time explaining to his superiors how he managed to crack a case without involving Ralph. To relax himself, Bill enjoyed snacking on what something most people would not eat?

Fly by Night

A700.   B-27

A701.   The Bomber's Bar

The Greatest American Hero

A702.   A strong moral character, integrity, and a healthy idealism

A703.   "The Jammies"

A704.   *The Daily Galaxy*

A705.   Dog biscuits

Hardcastle and McCormick
ABC, 1983–86

Q706. Milton C. Hardcastle was a judge known for his harsh courtroom sentences and Mark McCormick was a two-time loser up for his third offense. To avoid a prison term, Mark joined the judge in an effort to bring to justice the criminals who were tried but were set free by technicalities. The judge had a nickname that he received while serving on the bench. What was it?

Q707. Mark also had a nickname, but his was associated with stealing cars. He was not known for his driving skills and the nickname reflected it. What was it?

Hart to Hart
ABC, 1979–84

Q708. Jennifer and Jonathan Hart were a wealthy couple who helped people in trouble. Jonathan, the owner of Hart Industries, and Jennifer, a former journalist, met in London, married, and honeymooned in California's Napa Valley. They stayed in room 7 of what inn?

Q709. Jennifer was born in Hillhaven, Maryland, and attended the Gresham Prep School. At that time she also had a favorite horse on her father's ranch. What did she call the horse?

Q710. Jennifer tended to get a little tipsy from champagne and frequently lunched at La Scala's Restaurant. She also played a party hostess on what favorite daytime TV drama?

Hawaiian Eye
ABC, 1959–63

Q711. Tracy Steele, Tom Lopaka, and Gregg MacKenzie were private detectives called "The Eyes," a shortened name for their company. What was the exact name of their firm?

Q712. The Eyes operated from the Hilton Hawaiian Village Hotel where their friend and sometimes assistant, Cricket Blake, worked. Cricket ran the gift shop in the hotel. What was her business called?

Hardcastle and McCormick

A706.   "Hardcase"

A707.   "Skid"

Hart to Hart

A708.   The O'Berge Inn

A709.   Sweet Sue

A710.   *Doctors' Hospital*

Hawaiian Eye

A711.   Hawaiian Eye—Investigation-Protection

A712.   Cricket's Corner

Hawaiian Eye *continued*

Q713. In addition to the gift shop, Cricket also earned money as a singer at the hotel. In what room did Cricket perform?

Q714. Each of the detectives had an eye for beautiful women and Tom and Tracy had a special nickname for Cricket. What did they call her?

In the Heat of the Night
NBC/CBS, 1988–95

Q715. Bill Gillespie is the white police chief of Sparta, Mississippi, and Virgil Tibbs is his black chief of detectives. Tibbs is married to Aletha, a schoolteacher; Gillespie is a widower who, before he began romancing Harriet DeLong, a black city councilwoman, dated JoAnn St. John, a former prostitute who was trying to turn her life around. JoAnn worked at Gillespie's favorite eatery. What was it?

Q716. Gillespie enjoys hunting in his spare time and sometimes rides with his hunting dog in his patrol car. What is the dog's name?

Q717. Parker Williams is one of Gillespie's deputies. He has three cats and his favorite watering hole is the Big T Truck Stop. Name at least two of his cats.

The Invaders
ABC, 1967–68

Q718. The aliens (called Invaders) are here; one man, David Vincent, has seen them. Could he convince a disbelieving world that the nightmare had already begun? Returning home from a business trip late one night and getting tired, David had taken an exit off Highway 166 and found himself on a desolate country road. It was here that David had his close encounter. At what time of morning did this happen?

A713.   The Shell Lounge

A714.   "Lover"

In the Heat of the Night

A715.   The Magnolia Cafe

A716.   Roscoe

A717.   Old Man, Fuzz Face, Wrencher

The Invaders

A718.   4:20

The Invaders continued

Q719. The Invaders had taken human form and planned to assimilate into society. Their transformations were not always perfect and David knew their one flaw. What was it?

Q720. The Invaders were emotionless in any form, but some aliens developed emotions. What did the alien leaders call these outcasts?

The Islanders
ABC, 1960–61

Q721. Sandy Wade and Zack Malloy ran a small airline on an island in Sumatra. What was the name of this island ("whose chief natural resources are beautiful native girls")?

Q722. Argumentative partners Sandy and Zack were brought together by a mutual lady friend, Willie Vandeveer. Feeling both were going nowhere and needed a business, she was now their treasurer. Malloy and Company and Southern Cross were two of the names the trio rejected for their airline. What did they finally agree on for a name?

Q723. Shipwreck Callahan's was the American bar on the island. Shipwreck Callahan was the owner and the bank of Jakarta held the mortgage on the bar. What was Callahan's favorite drink to serve?

Jake and the Fatman
CBS, 1987–92

Q724. J.L. McCabe was first a district attorney, then a prosecuting attorney. J.L. was grossly overweight and had a similarly overweight dog named Max. McCabe had two nicknames; one of them was the "Fatman." What was the other?

Q725. J.L. was assisted by Jake Styles and Neely Capshaw. As a kid Jake had the nickname "Butchie," and the mythical Tom Cody was the star of his favorite TV show. What was it?

A719.   "Some of them have mutated hands; a crooked fourth finger."

A720.   Mutants

The Islanders

A721.   Ambowina

A722.   Lato Airways

A723.   A bamboo bomb

Jake and the Fatman

A724.   "Buster"

A725.   *Sky Hawk*

Johnny Bago
CBS, 1993

Q726. Johnny Tenuti was on the run from the mob for whacking a godfather's son. Though innocent, Johnny couldn't prove it unless he could find the real killer, a tattooed woman. He used the alias Johnny Bago and roamed the country in a Winnebago seeking to clear his name with the boys. What was the unique nameplate on the back of the bago?

Q727. Johnny had become a news item and had been featured on a TV reality show as a wanted criminal. What TV show had criminal profiles of him?

Q728. Beverly Florio was Johnny's ex-wife, a parole officer who was also after Johnny. She drove a beatup N.Y.P.D. station wagon and hoped to get Johnny before the mob did. The police car she drove was registered to what unit of the department?

Key West
Fox, 1993

Q729. After hitting a million-dollar lotto, Seamus O'Neill quit his job and moved to Key West to live like his hero, Ernest Hemingway. His joy was short lived when he got his first lotto check. How much was it for?

Q730. King Cole was Seamus's boss, the editor of the town's only newspaper. What was the name of the paper?

Q731. Gumbo owned the local hangout and had an alligator who "dreams of devouring a beautiful native girl who is helplessly tied to a tree." What had Gumbo named the alligator?

Q732. Savanagh was the local prostitute. She was proud to sell her body for money ("It was a lifelong dream of mine since childhood") and charged how much a night?

Johnny Bago

A726.   Travelin' Timberdoodle

A727.   *America at Large*

A728.   K-9 Squad

Key West

A729. $32.59

A730.   *The Meteor*

A731.   Tickled Pink

A732. $1,000

Knight Rider
NBC, 1982–86

Q733. KITT, the Knight Industries 2000, was a sleek car specially designed to battle crime. It could speak, had been programmed to protect human life, and was virtually indestructible. KITT could travel over any substance, even water. What system allowed this?

Q734. Being a car did limit KITT to where it could go. When neither Michael Knight, its driver, nor KITT could get into an area that needed investigating, what device did Michael use?

Q735. Before Wilton Knight perfected KITT, he produced KARR, an evil prototype that had no respect for human life. What did KARR stand for?

Life Goes On
ABC, 1989–93

Q736. The Thatchers were a Catholic family of five (Drew and Libby were the parents; Paige, Becca, and Corky their children), residing in the town of Glen Brook. Drew was a construction worker who quit his job for a better opportunity—to own his own business, a diner. For what construction company had he worked?

Q737. Libby was a singer and dancer who gave up her career to raise a family. She starred, for example, in an Off-Broadway production of *West Side Story*. What was her stage name at the time?

Q738. Libby was now with the Berkson and Berkson Ad Agency and, since going back to work, missed her favorite TV soap opera. What show was it?

Q739. Paige, Drew's somewhat rebellious daughter from a first marriage, was undecided about her future until she and a friend began their own construction company. What was the name of their business?

Knight Rider

A733. A third-stage aquatic synthesizer

A734. SID (Satellite Infiltration Drone)

A735. Knight Automated Roving Robot

Life Goes On

A736. Quentico

A737. Libby Dean

A738. *Forever and a Day*

A739. Darlin' Construction Company

Life Goes On continued

Q740. Becca was fifteen and a talented ballerina who hoped to one day become a writer. Because she had a tendency to write articles that are considered too controversial for her school newspaper at Marshall High, she turned to the school's forbidden tabloid. Name this paper.

Q741. Corky, afflicted with Down's syndrome, tried to be like other kids. Before attending Marshall High School, Corky was enrolled in an institution to help him function. What was the name of the school?

The Love Boat
ABC, 1977–87

Q742. The *Pacific Princess* was a luxury cruise ship that had been nicknamed "The Love Boat" by her crew. What company owned the ship?

Q743. Before it became the *Pacific Princess*, the ship was called the *Sun Princess* in the 1976 pilot film. In honor of the show's 1,000th guest star, the ship's name was changed once again. Name either the 1,000th guest or the ship's new moniker.

McMillan and Wife
NBC, 1971–76

Q744. When Sally, the wife of San Francisco Police Commissioner Stewart McMillan, began courses in gourmet cooking, she prepared meals Mac "loved." Name at least one of these gourmet meals.

Q745. Mildred was the McMillans' housekeeper. She called herself by a specific name. What was it?

Magnum, P.I.
CBS, 1980–88

Q746. Thomas Magnum, a former naval intelligence officer turned private detective, lived on the estate of pulp writer Robin Masters in return for providing its security. As a P.I., how much a day did Magnum charge?

A740. *The Underground Marshall*

A741. The Fowler Institute

The Love Boat

A742. Pacific Cruise Lines

A743. Lana Turner or the *Royal Princess*

McMillan and Wife

A744. Rattlesnake béarnaise or walnut casserole in goat butter

A745. "A Jack of all trades in the McMillan household."

Magnum, P.I.

A746. $200

Magnum, P.I. *continued*

Q747. Magnum was born in the town of Tidewater, Virginia, and had his first job delivering newspapers for the *Daily Sentinel*. What did Magnum earn a week at the time?

Q748. Magnum recorded his experiences as a detective, hoping to one day turn his notes into a book. He regularly mentioned what he was going to call the book. What was it?

Q749. Jonathan Higgins, the estate's major domo, was a survival expert with endless stories about his experiences during the war. Higgins had two dogs who helped him patrol the estate, Zeus and Apollo. By what nickname were they called?

Q750. Robin Masters was never seen. Higgins acted on Robin's behalf and Magnum suspected that Higgins was Robin but he couldn't prove it. What was the common nickname for Masters' estate?

Q75I. T.C. and Rick were Magnum's friends, who served with him in Vietnam. Rick tended bar and T.C. ran a helicopter charter service. What was the name of T.C.'s company?

Matlock
NBC/ABC, 1986–95

Q752. Ben Matlock is a rumpled Atlanta-based lawyer who has a record of successfully defending clients. He is also known for his high prices. How much does it cost to hire Ben?

Q753. Ben snacks on hot dogs at every opportunity and prefers to "wash it down" with soda. What flavor of soda does Ben drink?

Q754. Ben doesn't trust police labs and prefers to do his own investigating. What has he against police labs?

Q755. Ben rises every morning at five ("It's the best time for thinking") and is very strict about one thing which he prohibits in his office (and that even applies to his best-paying clients). What is it?

A747. $12 plus a penny for each paper sold

A748.   "How to Be a World Class Private Investigator."

A749.   "The Lads"

A750.   "Robin's Nest"

A751.   Island Hoppers

Matlock

A752. $100,000

A753.   Grape

A754.   "They're not working for my client."

A755.   Smoking

Max Headroom
ABC, 1987

Q756. In a future time, Network 23 was the top-rated TV station. Channel switching during commercials had become a major problem because it caused a dip in Network 23's ratings. There were a number of competing TV stations; name at least two.

Q757. Overweight or inactive people built up electrical charges; active people burned these charges off. To prevent channel switching, Network 23 began airing subliminal commercials that compressed thirty seconds into only three. These commercials violently stimulated the electrical charges in overweight and inactive people and caused them to explode (spontaneously combust). What were these commercials called?

Q758. Network 23 broadcasts via the Comstat 2058 Satellite. What was the network's slogan?

Melrose Place
Fox, 1991–

Q759. Young singles in an apartment complex at 4616 Melrose Place provide the setting. What is the local watering hole?

Q760. Sandy is an aspiring actress who had her first role in an unnamed horror flick. How does she describe her film debut?

Q761. Jane, a budding fashion designer, runs a small boutique. What is its name?

Midnight Caller
NBC, 1988–91

Q762. Jack Kilian was a former police inspector now hosting a radio call-in program, *Midnight Caller*. On what station did the show air?

Q763. The telephone number of the radio station was 555-TALK and it was located at 93.3 on the FM dial. By what name did Jack call himself on the air?

Max Headroom

A756. BBC 126, Planet Wide, Big Time TV, Channel 1111, PornoVision, Channel 28, Rubbish TV

A757. Blipverts

A758. "The Network That Means Business"

Melrose Place

A759. Shooters (a bar-poolroom)

A760. "Eight lines, two screams, and a topless scene."

A761. The Mart

Midnight Caller

A762. KCJM

A763. "The Nighthawk"

Moonlighting
ABC, 1985–89

Q764. Maddie Hayes was a model left penniless when her business manager embezzled her funds. Before she was able to sell a failed detective agency, one of her holdings, to raise money, David Addison talked her into saving it. She changed the name of the agency to Blue Moon Investigations and became a private detective. What was the agency's original name?

Q765. Maddie had appeared on the covers of such magazines as *Vogue* and *Glamour* and represented what product on TV?

Q766. "Do bears bear? Do bees bee?" was David's catchphrase. He also said that he is a capitalist ("I take my capital wherever I can get it"). David had an alliterative nickname for Maddie. What was it?

Murder, She Wrote
CBS, 1984–

Q767. Jessica Fletcher is a successful mystery author whose books include *All Fall Down Dead, The Corpse Wasn't There,* and *The Killer Called Collect.* What was the title of her very first book?

Q768. Jessica was a former English teacher whose late husband was named Frank. A central feature of her mysteries is a Saint-like character. Name him.

Q769. Living mainly in the small town of Cabot Cove, Maine, Jessica has two passions. One is riding her bicycle around town; what is the other?

Q770. When she is not in Maine, Jessica can be found in New York City, where she has an apartment at the Penfield House. She took the apartment to be near her publisher and to teach criminology at what college?

Moonlighting

A764. City of Angels Investigations

A765. Blue Moon Shampoo

A766. "Blondie Blonde"

Murder, She Wrote

A767. *The Corpse Danced at Midnight*

A768. Damian Sinclair

A769. Fishing

A770. Manhattan University

Naked City
ABC, 1958–63

Q771. "There are eight million stories in the Naked City. This has been one of them." These spoken words ended each episode with perhaps the most famous line in TV history. The Naked City was Manhattan, and programs were character studies of the people of a large metropolis. The police detectives of what New York City precinct were featured on the program?

Q772. Today, the New York City Police Department is known by the initials N.Y.P.D. But, on the series, different initials appeared on police vehicles. What were they?

Northern Exposure
CBS, 1990–95

Q773. Joel Fleischman is a misplaced medical school graduate who began his practice in Cicely, Alaska, a small town that bankrolled his studies. Joel attended Camp Indian Head as a kid, went to Richfield High School, and graduated from Columbia University Medical School. At what hospital did he do his internship?

Q774. Cicely has a population of 215 (counting Joel) and has an elevation of 6,572 feet. There has never been a doctor's office in Cicely, so Joel was given an abandoned building for his practice. What occupied the place before Joel?

Q775. Maggie O'Connell is Joel's landlady. She was born in Michigan and now owns a one-plane company. What is it called?

Q776. Cicely is virtually crime free. However, during the spring thaw, when the ice breaks, "people go crazy." What happens?

Q777. Maurice Minifield, a former NASA astronaut, founded the town of Cicely. The local paper is the Cicely *World Telegram* and Minifield Communications runs the only radio station. What is its nickname?

Naked City

A771. 65th

A772. P.D.N.Y.C. (Police Department of New York City)

Northern Exposure

A773. Beth Sinai

A774. Northwestern Mining

A775. O'Connell Air Taxi Service

A776. They steal things.

A777. "Great Bear Radio"

Perry Mason
CBS, 1957–63

Q778. Erle Stanley Gardner's brilliant criminal attorney, Perry Mason, came to TV in 1957. To contact Perry by phone, one simply called Hollywood 2-1799. If you wanted to meet with Mr. Mason, where would you find his office?

Q779. Perry seemed to be "all work and no play" but he did enjoy eating at what particular diner in Los Angeles?

Q780. While rarely seen consulting a law book, Perry did have a library, which was shown under the closing credits. Name one of the two books seen.

Picket Fences
CBS, 1992–

Q781. Rome, Wisconsin, seems like a charming little town, but behind its picket fences lie many strange things. Jimmy Brock is its sheriff and Max Stewart and Kenny Lacos are his deputies. Max is a beautiful brunette who doesn't seem like the type to kill, but when it comes to upholding the law, she will do what it takes. Name the two murderers she is famous for gunning down.

Q782. Jimmy is married to Jill and is the father of three children, Kimberly, Matthew, and Zachary. Jill is a private-practice doctor who is also on call where?

Q783. The *Herald* is the town's newspaper; Douglas Wambaugh is the outlandish defense attorney; and Henry Bone is the town's only judge. In what county are cases tried?

Police Woman
NBC, 1974–78

Q784. Pepper Anderson was a glamorous fashion model who, bored with her career, became a police officer to find more excitement in life. With what division of the L.A.P.D. did Pepper work?

Perry Mason

A778. Suite 904 in the Brent Building in Los Angeles

A779. McQuade's Bar and Grill

A780. *Corpus Juris*, Vol. 39 and Vol. 51

Picket Fences

A781. The Green Bay Chopper and the Cupid Killer

A782. Norwood Hospital

A783. Hogan County

Police Woman

A784. Criminal Conspiracy Division

Police Woman *continued*

Q785. When Pepper first joined the force, she was assigned to undercover work of a different kind. It was kind of tacky and Pepper didn't really like it. What job was it?

Q786. Pepper was a nickname and, although it was rarely mentioned, she did have a real first name. What was it?

Reasonable Doubts
NBC, 1991–93

Q787. Richard "Dicky" Cobb was a tough detective who is assigned by the D.A.'s office to assist Tess Kaufman, a hearing-impaired prosecuting attorney. Although knowing sign language, Cobb did not attend school to learn it. How did he learn sign?

Q788. Cobb's romantic interest was Kay Lockman, the owner of his favorite bar. Name this watering hole.

Remington Steele
NBC, 1982–86

Q789. Remington Steele did not actually exist. He was created by private investigator Laura Holt as "front man" to save her faltering business. An unknown thief crossed her path and to get out of a scrape, posed as Remington Steele. He later talked Laura into making him her partner. Before beginning her own business (Laura Holt Investigations), she was employed by what outfit?

Q790. As a kid Laura had the nickname "Binky," and *Atomic Man* was her favorite TV show. And, since a youngster "the Holt Curse" had followed her into adulthood. What was "the Holt Curse?"

Q791. Remington was a movie and TV fan and solved crimes based on old movie plots. When taking cases, Remington assumed names all taken from the films of his favorite actor. Who was it?

A785. Detective with the vice squad

A786. Lee Anne (but also mentioned as Suzanne)

Reasonable Doubts

A787. From his deaf father

A788. The Set Up Bar

Remington Steele

A789. Havenhurst Detective Agency

A790. A craving for chocolate that is difficult to control

A791. Humphrey Bogart

Remington Steele *continued*

Q792. The man who took the name of Remington Steele was born in Ireland and was apparently an orphan. He was taken in by a sophisticated thief and taught the fine art of crime. Who took Remington under his wing?

Richard Diamond, Private Detective
CBS/NBC, 1957–60

Q793. "A detective is only as good as his snitch," was the motto of Richard Diamond, a rugged private eye working out of New York City. How much did Diamond pay his snitches?

Q794. Richard called her "Samuel" and he had never seen her. She was Diamond's telephone answering service girl. What is the name of the company she ran?

Q795. The viewer had a slight advantage over Diamond in that a bit of Sam, mostly her very shapely legs, could be seen. First Mary Tyler Moore, then Roxanne Brooks played the role. What size stockings did "Samuel" wear?

The Roaring 20's
ABC, 1960–62

Q796. The Charleston Club on East 52nd Street was a hot nightspot owned by Pinky Pinkham and frequented by newspaper reporters Pat Garrison and Scott Norris. Pinky was also a singer at the club and she rarely used her real first name. What was it?

Q797. Scott and Pat were reporters who often played detective to get a story. What was their salary when the series began?

Q798. Scott and Pat worked for the *Record* and their favorite bar was located next to the Record Building. What was it called?

A792. Daniel Chalmers

Richard Diamond, Private Detective

A793. $10

A794. The Hi-Fi Answering Service

A795. Size 10 medium length

The Roaring 20's

A796. Delaware

A797. $40

A798. Chauncey's

Search
NBC, 1972–73

Q799.   Probe was a supercomputerized detective agency specializing in the recovery of whatever is missing ("If you lose it, we find it"). Based in Washington, D.C., Probe operated out of what organization?

Q800.   Hugh Lockwood, Nick Bianco, and Chris Grover were three highly skilled investigators who worked for Probe. Hugh's code was Probe One. What were the code names for Nick and Chris?

Q801.   Each agent had a superminiaturized transmitter/receiver surgically implanted in the ear. What was this device called?

Q802.   Sensing devices were implanted in agent's bodies and a body detector under their skin. Each agent also carried an ultraminiaturized TV camera capable of transmitting from any part of the world. How was the signal picked up by Probe Control?

77 Sunset Strip
ABC, 1958–64

Q803.   77 Sunset Strip was the business address of private detectives Stu Bailey and Jeff Spencer. Girls often said, "You're too cute to be a snoop," when they saw Jeff, who read *Playboy* magazine and was quite generous to his snitches. How much did he pay them?

Q804.   Dino's Lodge was located next to 77 Sunset Strip and Gerald Lloyd Kookson III, a.k.a. Kookie, was its parking lot attendant. Kookie drove a hot rod and used hip (for the time) terms like "Squaresville, Man." He also had what slang term for Stu and Jeff?

Q805.   Kookie had a flamboyant way of combing his hair that drove teenage girls crazy. Trouble was "Troublesville" and he had a term for pretty chicks. What was it?

Q806.   Suzanne Fabray worked the switchboard in office 103 at 77 Sunset Strip. What was the name of her company?

Search

A799. World Securities Corporation

A800. Nick was Omega Probe; Chris was Standby Probe.

A801. An Ear Check

A802. By Tele Communications Transatlantic Net via Tracking Station Niner Six Grid

77 Sunset Strip

A803. $50

A804. "Hey, Dad"

A805. "Dreamboats"

A806. The Sunset Answering Service

77 Sunset Strip continued

Q807. Dino's Lodge closed at two in the morning, and the Frankie Ortega Trio provided the supper club's music. Dino also had a business in the back of the lodge that catered to the pampered dogs of its patrons. What was it called?

Silk Stalkings
CBS, 1991–95

Q808. Rita Lee Lance and Chris Lorenzo are Florida police detectives who investigate society murders they call "Silk Stalkings." For what area of the Palm Springs Police Department do Rita and Chris work?

Q809. Rita and Chris's favorite sport is golf, and golfing great Sammy Snead is their hero. By what nickname do Rita and Chris call each other?

Sisters
NBC, 1991–

Q810. The lives of four close-knit sisters (Georgie, Teddy, Alex, and Frankie) are depicted on a weekly basis. All the sisters have male names. Why?

Q811. Their lives were made into a TV movie with the premise "Four sisters for each other forever." What was the movie called?

Q812. Georgie has a Ph.D. in anthropology but works as a real estate broker for what company?

Q813. Alex is the tight-fisted one of the family and was married to Wade until he left her for a younger woman. What leisure- time activity did Wade enjoy?

Q814. Teddy is the unstable sister and has held a number of jobs. She is a budding artist and fashion designer whose most famous client was First Lady Hillary Clinton. For what department store did Teddy design clothes?

A807.   Dino's Poodle Palace

Silk Stalkings

A808.   The Crimes of Passion Unit

A809.   "Sam"

Sisters

A810.   Their father had hoped for boys.

A811.   *A Sister's Love*

A812.   Maple Leaf Realties

A813.   Dressing in women's clothes

A814.   Bolzak's

Sisters continued

Q815. Frankie, the youngest of the four, is closest to Teddy. What nickname for Frankie as a youngster does Teddy still use?

South Beach
NBC, 1993

Q816. "I don't come cheap or easy," said Kate Patrick, a beautiful thief who worked for Roberts, a government agent who used criminals (like Kate) for undercover assignments. Kate was proud of her collection of exotic fish. What was the rarest fish she had in her aquarium?

Q817. Roxie, who dressed in various outfits and was called "Chameleon," operated a hotel for Roberts where Kate lives. What was its name?

Street Hawk
ABC, 1985

Q818. Operation Street Hawk was a top-secret project concerned with law enforcement. It was basically an attack motorcycle being tested by local police departments. Norman Tuttle created Street Hawk and Jesse Mach was his test pilot. Norman had added four high-volume air boxes and hyperthrust. Street Hawk normally cruised at 200 mph. What was its maximum speed?

Q819. Norman's dream was to see Street Hawk in every police department. He was also very protective of the bike and cringed at times at the way Jesse mishandled her. What "term of endearment" did Norman have for Street Hawk?

SurfSide 6
ABC, 1960–62

Q820. SurfSide 6 was a houseboat and the address of a detective agency owned by Dave Thorne, Sandy Winfield, and Ken Madison. Where in Miami Beach is the houseboat docked?

A815. "Stinkerbelle"

South Beach

A816. A Blue Phantom

A817. The Red Sands Hotel

Street Hawk

A818. 300 mph

A819. "My Baby"

SurfSide 6

A820. At Indian Creek

SurfSide 6 *continued*

Q821.   Daphne DeWitt Dutton, who lived on the neighboring yacht, was a beautiful jet setter and heir to the Dutton Racing Stables. What did she name the horse at the stables that she raised from a colt?

Q822.   Cha Cha O'Brien was the club singer at the Fontainebleau Hotel, located opposite SurfSide 6 on Ocean Avenue. In what room did she perform?

The Waltons
CBS, 1972–81

Q823.   Waltons Mountain in the Blue Ridge Mountains of Virginia was not owned by the Walton family ("we sort of hold it in trust"). What ancestor settled on the mountain in 1789?

Q824.   John and Olivia were the parents of six children and lived in Jefferson County. The oldest son, John-Boy, kept a journal about his family and yearned to be a writer. He began by establishing his own newspaper. What did he call it?

Q825.   Jason, the next son, was seeking musical fame. He attended the Clyneburg Conservatory and played with what band?

Q826.   The oldest girl, Mary Ellen, became a nursing student, while sister Erin first worked as a telephone operator. When World War II broke out, where did Erin find work?

Q827.   Jim-Bob and Elizabeth were the youngest Waltons. Jim-Bob was a twin and, while not specifically stated, his brother died at birth. Had he survived, what name would he have had?

Q828.   Ike Godsey owned the town's general store. The phone had three short and one long ring and Ike had a special hiding place for the store's keys. Where was it?

A821.   Par-a-Kee

A822.   The Boom Boom Room

The Waltons

A823.   Rome Walton

A824.   *The Blue Ridge Chronicle*

A825.   Bobby Bigelow and His Hayseed Gang

A826.   Pickett Metal Products Company

A827.   Joseph Zebulon

A828.   The coffee grinder

The Waltons continued

Q829. Miss Emily and Miss Mamie were spinster sisters who were friends of the Waltons. Although known bootleggers, they didn't tend to think of themselves as breaking the law. What did they call the moonshine they made?

Q830. The Waltons had a number of pets: a dog, a mule, a cow, a goat, a cat, and a peacock. Give the names of any two.

Q831. Charlottesville was the nearest major city and the White Arrow Bus Lines served the area. What were Jefferson County's neighboring towns?

Wonder Woman
ABC, 1976–79

Q832. Paradise Island, located in the Bermuda Triangle, was ruled by a race of Amazons who lived in peace. These women had incredible strength and the ability to run and jump at an accelerated speed. What was the first commandment of Paradise Island?

Q833. Amazons could find Paradise Island "because we know where it is." What prevented anyone else from finding this uncharted island?

Q834. Amazons wore bracelets made of what metal that can be found only on Paradise Island?

Q835. The bracelets possessed by Amazons were part of the process to help them deflect bullets. What other aspect, found only in an Amazon, could make her attempt "bullets and bracelets"?

Q836. If by chance an uninvited visitor came onto Paradise Island, the Amazons had the ability to erase that person's memory of them and of the island with a special drug. From what tree did this drug come?

A829. "Papa's Recipe"

A830. Reckless (dog), Blue (mule), Chance (cow), Myrtle (goat), Calico (cat), Rover (peacock)

A831. Hickory Creek and Waynesboro

Wonder Woman

A832. "To never tell anyone about it"

A833. Refraction of light

A834. Feminum

A835. "The Amazon mind is conditioned for athletic ability. Only we have the speed and coordination to attempt this."

A836. The Hybernia Tree

CHAPTER

3

Kid Shows, Science Fiction

Series and Westerns

The Adventures of Superboy
Syndicated, 1988–91

Q837. This series followed the adventures of Clark Kent before he became Superman and moved to Metropolis. For what organization did Clark work here, prior to his job with the *Daily Planet*?

Q838. Before relocating to Florida to take the job mentioned in the above question, Clark attended Schuster University and wrote for the school newspaper. What was it called?

Q839. Like almost everyone, Clark had to get up for work. At what time did his alarm clock ring?

Q840. Kryptonite, of course, is the one menace that can kill Clark. In this series, there was only one known supply of the green substance. Where was it?

The Adventures of Superman
Syndicated, 1953–57

Q841. In the classic opening theme, as the announcer intoned "More powerful than a locomotive," a diesel engine was seen (color episodes). What was the roadname of that engine?

The Adventures of Superboy

A837.　The Bureau of Extra Normal Matters

A838.　*The Herald*

A839.　6:30 A.M.

A840.　The Shift Military Institute

The Adventures of Superman

A841.　Southern Pacific

The Adventures of Superman *continued*

Q842. Clark worked for the *Daily Planet* so he could learn of fast-breaking stories and act quickly as Superman. How much did a copy of the paper cost?

Q843. Prior to becoming the editor of the *Daily Planet*, Perry White held two jobs. What were they?

Q844. Clark lived in a small apartment in Metropolis. What was the name of the hotel and what was his apartment number?

Alien Nation
Fox, 1989–90

Q845. Little Tencton, an area in Los Angeles, was where a group of aliens from the planet Tencton lived. Among them were George Francisco and his wife Susan. What was George's alien name?

Q846. The aliens were referred to as the Newcomers as well as by what slang term?

Q847. In order to reproduce, Newcomers required a husband, a wife, and a special mating alien. What was this special alien called?

Q848. Newcomer women were sexually aroused by what Earth TV public service announcement?

Andy's Gang
NBC, 1955–58

Q849. "I gotta gang, you gotta gang, everybody's gotta have a gang; but there's only one gang for me—good old Andy's Gang." Who could forget that great opening theme to this classic kid's show? Host Andy Devine most often began each episode with "Andy's Story Time." What was the title of that big book he opened before he read a chapter from it?

A842.   Five cents

A843.   Newspaper reporter, then mayor of Metropolis

A844.   The Standish Arms Hotel, Apartment 5H

Alien Nation

A845.   Neemo

A846.   "Slags"

A847.   A Binon

A848.   The piercing tone of an emergency broadcast test

Andy's Gang

A849.   *Andy's Stories*

Andy's Gang continued

Q850. There was also a regular weekly segment with Midnight the Cat and Squeaky the Mouse. What musical instrument did Squeaky play?

Q851. At the end of the program, before the closing theme, Andy appeared to bid farewell for this Saturday morning and to remind kids not to forget something. What was it?

Annie Oakley
Syndicated, 1954–57

Q852. Annie Oakley, TV's earliest heroine, invariably hit what she aimed at ("Once Annie aims at something it's a bullseye"). In the opening theme, she shot a hole in the center of what playing card?

Q853. Target and later Daisy were Annie's horses. Her brother, Tagg, also had a horse. What was its name?

Q854. Annie had a special area outside of town that she turned into a game preserve (Tagg's rabbit, Mr. Hoppity, lived there). What did Annie call this area?

Astro Boy
Syndicated, 1963

Q855. "Crowds will cheer you, you're a hero, go go Astro Boy." The theme hailed the exploits of the robot Astro Boy as he battled evil. Astro Boy, however, was created under tragic circumstances when a scientist lost his son in a car accident and created the robot in the boy's image. What was the boy's real name?

Q856. "I hearby christen thee my robot son, Astro Boy" was said by the real boy's father, Professor Boynton, when electricity gave the robot life one year later. The robot was taught and learned all there was to know, but it failed to mature. A disgusted Boynton sold the robot to a circus sideshow. Who bought Astro Boy?

A850.   The ukulele

A851.   Andy's closing speech: "Yes sir, we're pals and pals stick together. And now don't forget church or Sunday school…"

Annie Oakley

A852.   Nine of spades

A853.   Pixie

A854.   Annie's Ark

Astro Boy

A855.   Aster Boynton

A856.   The Great Catchatori

Astro Boy continued

Q857.   When Dr. Elefun discovered what happened he rescued Astro Boy from the circus by having a law passed that freed robots. What was this law called?

Q858.   Dr. Elefun had an I.Q. of 138 and headed the Institute of Science. Astro Boy had superhuman strength, super hearing, and rockets in his feet. How much horsepower did the rockets' motors produce to enable Astro Boy to fly?

Battlestar Galactica
ABC, 1978–79

Q859.   After their world was destroyed by the evil Cylons, a group of survivors banded together to follow the Galactica, a giant battlestar ship, as it searched for the planet Earth. How many ships were following the Galactica?

Q860.   The commander of the Galactica was Adama, who was assisted by his children, Starbuck, Apollo, and Athena. His wife, however, was killed in the final confrontation that destroyed their home planet. What was Adama's wife's name?

Q861.   Starbuck's romantic interest was the beautiful Cassiopea. She was a socialator (high-priced call girl) and objected to Starbuck smoking cigars. What did her name mean?

Q862.   The Galacticans' enemies were the Cylon warriors. What were these warriors called and what type of ships did they pilot?

Q863.   Adama lived on the planet Caprica, one of the twelve home planets that were destroyed. What was the mother planet called?

A857. The Robot Bill of Rights

A858. 100,000

Battlestar Galactica

A859. 220

A860. Lila

A861. "Fairy Queen"

A862. Raiders were the warriors; Vipers were their ships

A863. Cobor

The Beany and Cecil Show
ABC, 1963–67

Q864. Beany, the freckle-faced boy, and Cecil, the seasick sea serpent, assisted Horatio K. Huffenpuff, captain of the *Leakin' Lena*, as they sought adventure. Horatio possessed a trophy for what distinction?

Q865. He was voted villain of the year and he was the captain's enemy, "the do-badder who hates do-gooders." Who was he?

Q866. Cecil called himself "tall, green, and gruesome" and had a favorite TV star. Who was she?

The Big Valley
ABC, 1965–69

Q867. Victoria Barkley and her grown children, Jarrod, Heath, Nick, and Audra, owned the Barkley Ranch in the San Joaquin Valley in Stockton, California. The ranch comprised how many acres?

Q868. On the trail Heath Barkley was famous for what meal?

Q869. Heath's good luck charm was a bit unusual because if it were alive it could kill him. What was it?

Q870. Nick was the ranch foreman and an expert on horses. He was fond of one particular horse that he had had for a long time. What was its name?

Q871. Victoria also had a horse that she rode on a regular basis. What was the name of her horse?

Bonanza
NBC, 1959–73

Q872. Ben Cartwright and sons Adam, Hoss, and Little Joe owned the Ponderosa Ranch in the Comstock Lode Country near Virginia City, Nevada. It was a vast timberland ranch. How many square miles was it?

The Beany and Cecil Show

A864. "World's Greatest Liar"

A865. Dishonest John

A866. Dinah Shore

The Big Valley

A867. 30,000

A868. Bullfrog stew

A869. The rattler from a rattlesnake

A870. Coco

A871. Misty Girl

Bonanza

A872. 1,000

Bonanza *continued*

Q873. Ranch hands were always treated well by the Cartwrights and earned a decent wage. What was their pay?

Q874. Each of the Cartwright sons had a different mother. Adam was by Elizabeth Stoddard, Hoss by Inger Borgstrom, and Little Joe by Marie DeMarne. What was Hoss's first name (Hoss is his middle name and it was Swedish for a big friendly man)?

Q875. Ben rode a horse named Buck. Name Little Joe's and Hoss's horses.

Branded
NBC, 1965–66

Q876. "Branded, marked with a coward's shame. What do you do when you're branded and you know you're a man? Wherever you go for the rest of your life you must prove you're a man. Branded." Jason McCord, an ex-army captain, was branded "the coward of Bitter Creek" for deserting his troops during a Comanche attack. He had been knocked unconscious and woke up in a farmer's house some miles from the scene, unable to explain what happened. But because of Horace Greeley's newspaper columns about Jason's cowardice, Jason was also known by what two other names?

Q877. Jason was born in Washington, D.C., and attended West Point. What soon-to-become-famous general did Jason, a cadet, coach on his entrance exams?

Q878. The skills Jason learned in the army allowed him to establish a company with his grandfather, Gen. Joshua McCord. What did they call the business?

Bronco
ABC, 1958–60

Q879. Bronco Layne was "born down around the old Panhandle" and "there ain't a horse that he can't handle, that's how he got his name." Bronco served with the Texas Confederacy and had a reminder of the Battle of Elmira. What was it?

A873. $30 a month, a bunk, and beans

A874.   Eric

A875.   Cochise (Little Joe's horse) and Chuck (Hoss's horse)

Branded

A876.   "Yellow Tail" and "Yellow Belly"

A877.   George Armstrong Custer

A878.   McCord & McCord, Survey Engineers

Bronco

A879.   A cat he called Elmira

Bronco *continued*

Q880. Bronco also had a pocket watch that played what particular song when it was opened?

Q881. Inside the pocket watch was a picture of the only girl Bronco ever loved (they grew up in Texas together). Who was she?

Captain Scarlet and the Mysterons
Syndicated, 1967

Q882. Spectrum, a futuristic organization, had been established to safeguard the Earth. Where was Spectrum headquartered?

Q883. The Mysterons were aliens who declared war on Earth when they mistook an exploration of their planet by Spectrum as an unprovoked attack. What planet was Spectrum battling?

Q884. Captain Scarlet was Spectrum's chief operative and Colonel White was the organization's commander-in-chief. Other agents included Lieutenant Green, Captain Blue, and Captain Magenta. What did all Spectrum agents have in common?

Captain Video and His Video Rangers
DuMont, 1949–57

Q885. Captain Video was "The Guardian of the safety of the world." He operated from a secret mountain headquarters and battled Earth's enemies. Dr. Pauli was one of the captain's most diabolical nemeses. What society did Dr. Pauli head?

Q886. Commissioner Bell was the captain's superior. He was based on the 144th floor of what building in Planet City?

A880. "Deep in the Heart of Dixie"

A881. Redemption McNally

Captain Scarlet and the Mysterons

A882. Cloudbase

A883. Mars

A884. They are all named after the colors of the Spectrum.

Captain Video

A885. The Asteroidal Society

A886. The Public Safety Building

Captain Video continued

Q887.   When the series was broadcast live, action scenes from old theatrical films were shown to allow costume and set changes. The actors in these films were said to be video rangers fighting for justice. What device did Captain Video use to tune into these rangers in the field?

Cheyenne
ABC, 1956–63

Q888.   Cheyenne Bodie was the name a twelve-year-old boy, the survivor of an Indian massacre on a wagon train, took when he chose to leave the Cheyenne tribe that raised him. What Indian name did the boy have?

Q889.   A wanderer, the grown Cheyenne took whatever jobs he could find. He hoped one day to settle down. What were his plans when the time came?

Q890.   Cheyenne was trusted by Indian chiefs and could read smoke signals. On the right side of his holster he carried a gun; what did he have on the left side?

Colt .45
ABC, 1957–60

Q891.   Chris Colt was an undercover agent for the government who posed as a salesman for the Colt .45. By what other name was the gun known?

Q892.   The gun had a finely milled butt "that seems to jump in the hand." How much did a Colt .45 cost?

Q893.   Chris would not sell his demonstrators ("I'd be out of business if I did that"). Once a gun was ordered from Chris how long did it take before it arrived?

A887.   The Remote Carrier Delayed Circuit TV Screen

Cheyenne

A888.   Grey Fox

A889.   Buy a ranch and raise horses

A890.   A hunting knife

Colt .45

A891.   "The Peacemaker"

A892. $20

A893.   Six months

Dr. Quinn, Medicine Woman
CBS, 1993–

Q894. Michaela Quinn is a doctor in Colorado Springs in 1865, distrusted by most of the townspeople (who don't cotton to female doctors). This is no surprise to Michaela, who had a difficult time finding a medical school back east that would admit a woman. What school did Michaela attend?

Q895. The local Cheyenne Indians think Michaela is "a crazy white woman" because "only white men make medicine." Everything changes when she saves the life of the Cheyenne chief. What Indian name does the chief give her?

Dudley Do-Right of the Mounties
ABC, 1969–70

Q896. Dudley Do-Right was a simple-minded Mountie with the Canadian Mounted Police in North Alberta. He was honest to a fault and had been called "the man who can do no wrong." Dudley, however, became a disgrace to the Mounties one night at dinner for doing what despicable deed?

Q897. Sawmill owner Snidley Whiplash was "that meaner than mean, downright villainous, no good villain of the Northwest" who was constantly pursued by Dudley. He also had this uncontrollable urge to do something that could cost Inspector Ray K. Fenwick's daughter, Nell, her life. What was it?

The Eighth Man
Syndicated, 1965

Q898. "Quick call Tobor, the Eighth Man, the mightiest robot of them all" the theme exclaimed when evil threatened the Earth. Mr. Tobor, as he was called, was a private detective who was actually a robot created by Professor Genius. Tobor worked in Metro City and was a police officer before he was "killed" by Saucer Lip. Who was this police officer?

Dr. Quinn, Medicine Woman

A894. The Women's Medical College of Pennsylvania

A895. "Medicine Woman"

Dudley Do-Right of the Mounties

A896. He ate peas with a knife—"something a mountie would never do."

A897. Tying ladies to railroad tracks

The Eighth Man

A898. Peter Brady (Professor Genius embodied Brady's life force into that of the robot)

The Eighth Man continued

Q899. Mr. Tobor was head of the Tobor Detective Agency and often worked with the police department. Who was its chief?

Q900. Tobor had to take an energy booster to maintain his strength when he battled evil, such as Intercrime: Based on Intercrime Island, it was a threat to the safety of the world. Its symbol was a dagger plunged into the world. Who was its head?

The Flintstones
ABC, 1960–66

Q901. Fred and Wilma Flintstone and neighbors Betty and Barney Rubble resided in the town of Bedrock in the year 1,000,040 B.C. Fred and Barney toiled at the Slaterock Gravel Company. Before being laid off and finding a job with Fred's company, Barney worked for a rival outfit. What was it?

Q902. Fred and Barney were members of the Bedrock Quarry baseball team and their favorite TV show was *Jay Bond-rock*. The two also enjoyed bowling and were members of what lodge?

Q903. Barney and Betty had a pet Hoparoo called Hoppy while Fred and Wilma had a six-foot-tall, purple-with-black-spots pet named Dino. What kind of dinosaur was Dino?

Q904. Fred loved to eat, and although Wilma "fixes the best dodo bird in Bedrock," his favorite meal was something else. Name it.

George of the Jungle
ABC, 1967–70

Q905. In Africa lived George of the Jungle, a mighty hero who didn't know the meaning of the word fear ("But George can look it up"). What province in Africa did George protect?

A899. Chief Fumble Thumbs

A900. Dr. Spectre

The Flintstones

A901. The Pebble Rock and Gravel Company

A902. The Royal Order of the Water Buffalo

A903. Snarkasaurus

A904. Bronto Burgers

George of the Jungle

A905. The Mbweebee Valley

George of the Jungle continued

Q906. Rather naive, George had a problem with trees—he crashed into them when swinging from vine to vine like Tarzan. He had an ape named Ape and a mate called Ursula, as well as what prized possession?

The Ghost Busters
CBS, 1975–76

Q907. Spenser and Kong were ghost busters. They were assisted by a trained gorilla named Tracy and attempted to rid people's lives of ghosts with a ray gun–like weapon. What was it called?

Q908. The trio operated from a rather run-down office building that looked like it was about to be condemned. They took orders from a never-seen superior via a tape recording (as on *Mission Impossible*). Who was their boss?

The Guns of Will Sonnett
ABC, 1967–69

Q909. Jeff Sonnett had never seen his father, James; Jeff's grandfather, Will Sonnett, was determined that the two meet. A trek was begun to find James, a wanted gunman and killer, who deserted his family twenty years earlier (1852) after his wife died while giving birth. Will took on the responsibility of raising Jeff. Where did the Sonnetts live at this time?

Q910. The road Will and Jeff traveled was a difficult one because James was unaware that his kin were seeking him. While James may have been thought of as a killer, he aided people in trouble, and would kill only in self-defense. He carried with him a gold watch that was given to him by Will. What was the inscription in it?

Q911. Will was fast on the draw and James showed promise; "Trouble is, he left before I taught him half what I know." When faced with an opponent, Will would comment, "They say James is fast. Well, he ain't, I am." He ended each statement with what famous four-word catchphrase?

A906. His rhinestone yo-yo

The Ghost Busters

A907. A Ghost Dematerializer

A908. Mr. Zero

The Guns of Will Sonnett

A909. Bensfort, Wyoming

A910. "To James From His Loving Father"

A911. "No brag, just fact"

Have Gun—Will Travel
CBS, 1957–62

Q912. "Have Gun—Will Travel reads the card of a man, a knight without armor in a savage land." The words of the theme told of Paladin, a fast gun for hire who operated out of what hotel in San Francisco?

Q913. Paladin had box seats at the opera house, enjoyed fine food, smoked expensive cigars, and has an eye for the ladies. He also collected chessmen and had one rule. What was it?

Q914. A graduate of West Point, Paladin had a talent with a gun. He often read out-of-state newspapers and sent his calling card to people he felt might need his help. What was his fee?

Hotel de Paree
CBS, 1959–60

Q915. A man known only as Sundance was an ex-gunfighter turned lawman in Georgetown, Colorado in the 1870s. He turned his life around after serving a prison term and was now partners with Annette Devereaux in the Hotel de Paree, a fancy hotel and gambling hall. From what town and state did Sundance hail?

Q916. Also known as the Sundance Kid, he had a gun but would wear it only when necessary. He also sported a black Stetson with a hatband of small, highly polished mirrors that, when the sun shown on them, blinded opponents in gunfights. How many mirrors were on the hatband?

Q917. Sundance carried a Colt .45, had a knack for whittling and a dog who was always by his side. What was the dog's name?

Have Gun—Will Travel

A912. The Carlton

A913. "Never to go anyplace without my gun."

A914. $1,000

Hotel de Paree

A915. Tombstone, Arizona

A916. Ten

A917. Useless

Howdy Doody
NBC, 1947–60

Q918. While Buffalo Bob Smith tried to keep the peace in Doodyville, the nasty Phineas T. Bluster attempted to see that people had no fun. His assistant was Chief Thunderthud. To what Indian tribe did the chief belong?

Q919. Howdy Doody and his brother were born in Doodyville, Texas, on December 27, 1941, to parents who earned a living by performing chores for the ranch owner. What did Mr. and Mrs. Doody name Howdy's brother?

Isis
CBS, 1975–78

Q920. "O Mighty Isis" were the words Andrea Thomas spoke to become Isis, a daring defender of the underdog. Andrea had the power to become Isis by the magic of something she found while on an expedition in Egypt. What was it?

Q921. When Andrea became Isis, she was able to soar and had power over animals and control over the elements of earth, sea, and sky. When not battling evil, she was teaching what subject in high school?

Q922. Rick Mason, Andrea's friend, was a teacher and boating enthusiast who was unaware of her secret alias. What was his boat called?

Jeff's Collie
CBS, 1954–57

Q923. Jeff Miller lived on a farm in Calverton with his widowed mother, Ellen, and grandfather, George, who was affectionately called "Gramps." Jeff's dog, Lassie, was inherited from a neighbor. What was the neighbor's name?

Q924. A volunteer fireman and head of the school board, Gramps was born on the land he owned and on which he raised his family. He also had a term for people who irritated him. What was it?

Howdy Doody

A918. The Ooragnak Tribe (Ooragnak is Kangaroo spelled backwards)

A919. Double Doody

Isis

A920. A magic amulet

A921. Science

A922. *Star Tracker*

Jeff's Collie

A923. Homer Carey

A924. "Pusillanimous Polecat"

Jeff's Collie *continued*

Q925. Jeff and his friend, Porky Brockway, were blood brothers. Porky had a dog named Pokey, and Porky and Jeff had a special signal for each other. What was it?

Q926. Porky was overweight; his parents were on the hefty side; and Pokey, a basset hound, could have lost some poundage. What was Pokey's official name?

The Jetsons
ABC, 1962–63

Q927. The Jetsons were a twenty-first-century family. George and Jane were the parents, and Judy and Elroy were their children. In what housing complex did the family live?

Q928. George was in the army reserve (U.S. Space Guards Division) and worked for Spacely Space Sprockets. How many sprockets a day did the company produce?

Q929. Fifteen-year-old Judy had a talking diary she called Di Di and attended what school?

Q930. Elroy, her eight-year-old brother, had a dog named Astro and was a member of the Little Dipper League baseball team. What grammar school did he attend?

Johnny Ringo
CBS, 1959–60

Q931. Johnny Ringo was a gunfighter who went on the other side of the law to become sheriff of Velardi, Arizona. Johnny believed that the town hired his guns, not him, because his reputation was known from the Gulf to the Pacific Ocean. How much a month did he earn as sheriff?

Q932. Johnny had an unusual gun, a variation on the French firearm, the Le Met Special. It was designed by his friend, Cason Thomas, "to even up the odds." The gun looked like a regular Colt .45 but it had a separate barrel located under the standard one. What type of bullet did this barrel fire?

A925. "Eee-ock-eee"

A926. Pokerman III

The Jetsons

A927. The Sky Pad Apartments

A928. Three million

A929. Orbit High

A930. The Little Dipper School

Johnny Ringo

A931. $200

A932. A .410 shotgun shell

Land of the Lost
NBC, 1974–77

Q933. Forest ranger Rick Marshall and his children, Will and Holly, were rafting down the Colorado River when they were caught in a time vortex and transported to a land of prehistoric creatures. When the Marshalls found they could not escape, they established a home in a cave. What did they call their home?

Q934. Strange pyramid-like triangles controlled this alien land, and inside them were colored crystals that could open a time doorway to freedom if the right sequence could be found. What were these triangles called?

Lawman
ABC, 1958–62

Q935. "The Lawman came with the sun; there was a job to be done; so they sent for the badge and the gun of the Lawman." The man is Dan Troop, the marshal of Laramie, Wyoming, a town that "is tough on lawmen and horse thieves." When living back in Texas, Dan was the marshal of Abilene and became a legend. What was he called?

Q936. The Birdcage Saloon was the town's watering hole and the Blue Bonnet Cafe was the eatery. What was the name of the local newspaper?

Lost in Space
CBS, 1965–68

Q937. An attempt to explore a new planet failed when the space ship was thrown off course and stranded its crew and passengers. Donald West was the ship's pilot and the Robinson family (John, Maureen, and children Judy, Will, and Penny) were on board. Also there was Zachary Smith, an agent who sabotaged the ship. John was a professor of astrophysics and Maureen was a biochemist who was the first woman in U.S. history to do something. What was it?

Land of the Lost

A933.   High Bluff

A934.   Pylons

Lawman

A935.   "The Fast Gun From Texas"

A936.   *The Laramie Weekly* or *The Laramie Free Press* (as seen in the pilot)

Lost in Space

A937.   Pass the International Space Administration's grueling, emotionally draining test for intergalatic flight

Lost in Space *continued*

Q938. Penny, with an I.Q. of 147, was interested in zoology; Will held the highest average in the history of his school; and Judy had high hopes of doing something. For what did she "heroically postpone all hopes"?

Q939. Donald West "rocketed the scientific world with his theory of other planets' fitness for human habitation." From what school did he graduate?

Q940. "Bucket of Bolts" and "Pot-bellied pumpkin" were two of the "terms of endearment" Col. Zachary Smith used for the ship's environmental control robot. Smith saw the robot as a slave and had what regular nickname for it?

Q941. The Robot did object to Smith's demands and told him "My computer is not programmed for day and night work. I need eight hours rest like other robots." How did the Robot defend itself?

Maverick
ABC, 1957–62

Q942. "Who is the tall dark stranger there, Maverick is the name..." for brothers Bart and Bret, just this side of honorable gentlemen gamblers who roamed the Old West in search of rich prey. Their daddy, Beauregard "Pappy" Maverick, left each of his sons two things: profound words of wisdom ("Never hold a kicker and never draw to an inside straight") and what else?

Q943. It was against a Maverick's principle to drink alone and the boys had one serious vice. What was it?

Q944. Cousin Beau was the "white sheep" of the family, bringing honor to the Maverick name when he was credited with capturing a Union general during the Civil War. He also rode a horse with a rather unusual name. What was it?

A938. "A career in the musical comedy field"

A939. The Center for Radio Astronomy

A940. "Booby"

A941. With electrical discharges

Maverick

A942. A $1,000 bill

A943. Curiosity

A944. Gumlegs

The Marvel Super Heroes
Syndicated, 1965

Q945. "The Incredible Hulk," "Iron Man," "Captain America," "Sub Mariner," and "The Mighty Thor" were adapted to TV in animated form on this series. Donald Blake was the secret identity of the Mighty Thor, who had superhuman strength and the abilities of a Norse God. He also had a virtually indestructible throwing weapon. What was it called?

Q946. "When Captain America throws his mighty shield, all those who chose to oppose his shield must yield; and the red, the white, and the blue will come true when Captain America throws his mighty shield." Captain America, who stood six feet two and weighed 240 pounds, posed as an army private. He had abilities in speed and strength and his weapon was his shield. What name did he use as a cover?

Q947. Industrialist Tony Stark was secretly Iron Man. He wore an electronically powered suit of armor which increased his strength to superhuman levels. With the armor he stood six feet four inches tall. How much did he weigh?

The Mickey Mouse Club
ABC, 1955–59

Q948. "Who's the leader of the club that's made for you and me?" The opening line of the theme meant it was time for a daily visit with the Mouseketeers. Jimmie Dodd led the festivities, and each weekday was devoted to a specific subject (for example, Monday was "Fun With Music Day"). Name the other four days' shows.

Q949. "Time to twist our Mousekedial to the right and the left with a great big smile. This is the way we get to see a Mouse Cartoon for you and me." Finish the line that would open the Mickey Mouse Treasure Mine.

The Marvel Super Heroes

A945. Mjolnir, his enchanted hammer

A946. Steve Rogers

A947. 640 pounds

The Mickey Mouse Club

A948. Tuesday was Guest Star Day; Wednesday was Anything Can Happen Day; Thursday was Circus Day; Friday was Talent Roundup Day

A949. "Meeska, Mooseka, Mouseketeer, Mouse Cartoon Time Now Is Here."

The Monroes
ABC, 1966–67

Q950. Clayt, Kathleen, Amy, and twins Jefferson and Fennimore Monroe were orphaned children who settled in "Pa's Valley," a patch of wilderness in Wyoming to which their father, Albert, laid claim in 1866. What item of Albert's marked the claim?

Q951. While the Monroes called it "Pa's Valley," ranchers Barney Wales and Major Mapoy called it by its actual name. What is the official name of the valley?

National Velvet
NBC, 1960–62

Q952. Twelve-year-old Velvet Brown dreamed of owning a horse and training it for the Grand National Steeplechase. Part of her dream came true when she won a beautiful chestnut thoroughbred in a raffle. While Velvet (and everyone else) called the horse King, that was not his full name. What was it?

Q953. Velvet won several local competitions with King, including the Junior Hurdles. The horse was not hard to train, but Velvet did have one serious problem. What was it?

Q954. The Brown family owned a dairy farm in an area called the Valley. They sold their milk in neighboring Flintwood at what dairies?

Pistols 'n' Petticoats
CBS, 1966–67

Q955. Wretched, Colorado, was a wild and woolly town with a sheriff, Harold Sykes, but it was the Hanks family who maintained the law and order. Harold has instituted an antilittering ordinance called "Wretched Beautiful." How much was the fine for breaking the law?

The Monroes

A950.   His army belt buckle

A951.   Bear Valley

National Velvet

A952.   Blaze King

A953.   Breaking him to saddle

A954.   The Winters Dairies

Pistols 'n' Petticoats

A955.   Fifty cents

Pistols 'n' Petticoats continued

Q956. Henrietta Hanks was a widow with a daughter named Lucy, and lived on a ranch with Henrietta's mother and father. Henrietta "could fire a gun with one hand milking a goat and hit a coyote on the run." Andrew, her father, "kept his gun in trim; nobody messed around with him," and had a mule and a pet wolf. The mule was Molly, but what was the wolf named?

Planet of the Apes
CBS, 1974

Q957. Pete Burke and Alan Virdon were the U.S. astronauts marooned on a planet of highly intelligent apes in this TV adaptation of the feature films. Here Pete and Alan had crashlanded in an area that was previously called California. What had the ape leaders renamed it?

Q958. Alan and Pete believe that the only way to return to their time was by reversing the ship's magnetic disc, which recorded the flight. They had two problems with this theory. One was finding a computer; what was the other?

Punky Brewster
NBC/Syndicated, 1984–88

Q959. Punky Brewster was a seven-year-old girl, abandoned by her parents but adopted by a gruff photographer named Henry Warnimont. Although called "Gunky" Brewster at school, this adorable little girl had a real first name. What was it?

Q960. "That's Punky Power!" was one of Punky's catchphrases. What was "Punky Power"?

Q961. Margaux Kramer, Punky's very rich and spoiled girlfriend, took lessons from her mother on how to fire servants. She felt that the closest she would ever come to poverty was when she visited Punky at home. Margaux had a collection of dolls and one in particular was her favorite, a dancing ballerina that played what song that comforted her when she was sad?

A956.   Bowzer

Planet of the Apes

A957.   Central City

A958.   A human intelligent enough to build a ship

Punky Brewster

A959.   Penelope

A960.   "No matter how bad things look, everything will be all right."

A961.   "Beautiful Dreamer"

Quantum Leap
NBC, 1989–93

Q962. Dr. Samuel Beckett created Quantum Leap as a means of traveling through time. It was a top secret government project and was hidden in the New Mexico desert thirty miles from what town?

Q963. A system malfunction had trapped Sam in time and he could travel only within thirty years of his own lifetime. In his "leaps," Sam assumed the identities of people he had never known, to correct a mistake in their lives. Where did these people bide their time while Sam was assuming their identity?

Q964. Al Calavicci was a project observer whose holographic image appeared to Sam through brainwave transmissions. Sam was the only person who was supposed to see Al, but this was not so. Who else could see Al?

Q965. Sam had a specific reason for creating Quantum Leap and spent over a billion dollars developing it. What was the reason?

Quark
NBC, 1978

Q966. Betty I and Betty II were the copilots of a galaxy scow piloted by Adam Quark. Betty II was a clone of Betty I. Where was the cell taken from Betty I to create Betty II?

Q967. The ship Adam piloted patrolled the deep regions of space picking up the trash of other planets in the United Galaxies. How much compacted trash could Adam's ship hold?

Rango
ABC, 1967

Q968. "I'm Rango, just Rango, Texas Ranger" said Rango when asked his name. He was dimwitted, slow on the draw, and a major headache to his captain. In what Texas Ranger outpost was Rango stationed?

Quantum Leap

A962. Destiny County

A963. The Waiting Room at the Quantum Leap complex

A964. Dogs, certain children, and mentally unstable people

A965. "To make the world a better place and to make right what was once wrong."

Quark

A966. Under her fingernail

A967. 200,000 pounds

Rango

A968. Gopher Gulch

Rango continued

Q969. Rango believed that a law-abiding town is a happy town and had made eighty-four proclamations. Number one was "No guns allowed in town." What was number 84?

Rocky and His Friends
ABC, 1959–61

Q970. Twenty-nine people resided in Frostbite Falls, Minnesota. Two of them were Rocky the Flying Squirrel and his dimwitted friend, Bullwinkle the Moose. The town was serviced by the Union Pathetic Railroad and had only one movie theater, the Bijou. What was the first film shown at the theater?

Q971. Each year Rocky and Bullwinkle vacationed on "the wettest, soggiest, dreariest place on earth." What was this location?

Q972. Rocky was the all-American squirrel and wore an aviator's cap. He also said what (his catchphrase) when something went wrong?

Q973. It was difficult for Bullwinkle to follow the story and be part of it at the same time, and he relied on the show's narrator to help him. Through this narration Bullwinkle learned that his uncle discovered something that was now his claim to fame. What was it?

Q974. Dastardly Boris Badanov was "the world's lowest snake in the grass." He and his villainous assistant, Natasha, worked for Mr. Big (a midget who casts a giant shadow) and operated from where?

Saved by the Bell
NBC, 1989–

Q975. Kelly, Jesse, Lisa, Zack, Screech, and Slater are the featured students at Bayside High School in what fictional town in California?

A969.   "No whistling at girls on the street"

Rocky and His Friends

A970.   *A Trolley Named Tallulah*

A971.   An island called Moosylvania

A972.   "Hoakie Smokes"

A973.   A metal called Upsadaisium

A974.   The Old Bleakley House

Saved by the Bell

A975.   Palisades

Saved by the Bell continued

Q976. The Max is the after-school hangout and Kelly worked there as a waitress. Kelly knows she is very beautiful but fears someone will discover she is not perfect. What does she dread someone will learn about her?

Q977. Lisa loves shopping ("Lisa is my name and shopping is my game") and claims she has an ability no one else has. What is it?

Q978. Zack is the rich preppy student who became Principal Richard Belding's "Zack Ache" for all the aggravation he has caused with his pranks. One was a chance to make money by issuing the Girls of Bayside High Swimsuit Calendar. Kelly, Jesse, and Lisa were featured as month girls. Name the months each was a "Miss."

Q979. Screech was a fifth runner-up in an ALF lookalike contest and has a robot named Kevin as well as a dog, roach, mouse, lizard, spider, and two rats. Give the names for any two of these pets.

Sheena, Queen of the Jungle
Syndicated, 1956–57

Q980. Sheena was a female version of Tarzan, and the show featured Irish McCalla as the shapely blond jungle goddess. Like Tarzan, Sheena had a simian companion. What was his name?

Q981. And, like Tarzan, who had Jane, Sheena had a male friend, a white trader who assisted her. Name him.

Space 1999
Syndicated, 1975–77

Q982. It was the year 1999 and the moon had been blasted out of its orbit. Moonbase, as it was called, was now home to the 311 men and women assigned to it. John Koenig was the commander and Dr. Helena Russell the chief medical officer. As the moon drifted in space, the Earthlings encountered life forms from other planets. What did aliens call the residents of Moonbase Alpha?

A976.   She wears a retainer at night.

A977.   To guess the contents of a gift package without opening it.

A978.   Kelly was "Miss November"; Jesse "Miss July"; Lisa "Miss October"

A979.   Hound Dog (dog), Herbert (roach), Arnold (mouse), Oscar (lizard), Ted (spider)

Sheena, Queen of the Jungle

A980.   Chim

A981.   Bob Rayburn

Space 1999

A982.   Alphans

Space 1999 continued

Q983. Maya was an alien who became a member of Moonbase Alpha in second-season episodes. She was a metamorph, able to assume any form. From what planet did Maya come?

Space Rangers
CBS, 1993

Q984. In the year 2104 a renegade band of Space Rangers battles evil throughout the universe. John Boon is the captain and his crew includes Doc, Jo Jo, and Zylyn. Doc is the ship's repairman and has seven synthetic body parts. What do Boon and Jo Jo call him?

Q985. They don't tell us what a Zulu is, but it is the favorite drink of the Space Rangers. Where do they like taking their liquid refreshment?

Q986. The Space Rangers are fearless and will battle any enemy that poses a threat to Earth. They live and die by their motto. What is it?

Q987. Jo Jo and Zylyn are both aliens who assist Boon. Zylyn is a master at Zylyusian Flute Sword (like Earth dueling) and Jo Jo is a tall, blond bombshell from a planet where men are wimps. From what planets are Zylyn and Jo Jo?

Sugarfoot
ABC, 1957–60

Q988. A cowboy one grade lower than a tenderfoot was called a sugarfoot. Tom Brewster, a sugarfoot looked upon as a gullible greenhorn by the local roughnecks, was hoping to become a lawyer. All he wanted to do was study his law books. What law book does Tom carry with him?

Q989. Tom felt that guns were "tools of the devil" and that "shootin' ain't always the answer." He was also opposed to alcohol, but did frequent saloons. What drink did he always order?

A983. Psychon

Space Rangers

A984. "Tin Man"

A985. Geno's Bar.

A986. "Into the Jaws of Hell for Justice"

A987. Zylyn is from Grakka; Jo Jo from New Venus

Sugarfoot

A988. *Blackstone's Commentary*, vol. 9

A989. "Sarsaparilla with a touch of cherry"

Time Trax
Syndicated, 1993–95

Q990. Darien Lambert is a cop from the future (born on August 17, 2160) who has been sent back in time to 1993 to capture criminals who escape from their futures to our past. With what futuristic organization is Darien associated?

Q991. Police officers of the future, such as Darien, still use guns, but they are not types that kill; they immobilize suspects. What are these guns called?

Q992. Darien is assisted by SELMA, a holographic image that can give him any information that he requires. What does SELMA stand for?

Walker, Texas Ranger
CBS, 1993–

Q993. Cardell Walker is a Texas Ranger with the Department of Public Safety. Although he invariably exceeds his authority, his superiors admit that he is good. What is the name of Walker's horse?

Q994. Alexandra "Alex" Cahill is the prosecuting attorney and believes there is a special place in heaven for Walker. She helps him "so cases will not fall through the cracks of the legal system." Name her horse.

Yancy Derringer
CBS, 1958–59

Q995. Yancy Derringer, a former Confederate soldier, worked undercover for John Colton to help end the rising tide of crime, and was assisted by Pahoo, a nonspeaking Indian. What weapon did Pahoo carry with him at all times?

Q996. Yancy was born on a plantation in Louisiana and owned a riverboat. Name both the plantation and the riverboat.

Q997. He also had a dog and dressed in fancy "duds." Name the dog and the store at which Yancy bought his clothes.

Time Trax

A990. The Fugitive Retrieval System

A991. The Pellet Projection Tube

A992. Specified Encapsulated Limited Memory Archive

Walker, Texas Ranger

A993. Cookie

A994. Amber

Yancy Derringer

A995. A shotgun

A996. Waverly Plantation; the *Sultana*

A997. Old Dixie; Devereaux's Gentleman's Apparel

Zorro
ABC, 1957–59

Q998. Zorro, alias Don Diego, was the mysterious defender of the oppressed in Old Los Angeles. What old proverb prompted Don Diego to adopt the guise of Zorro (the Fox)?

Q999. Zorro was famous for carving his trademark Z. On what object did Zorro put his first Z?

Q1000. Sergeant Garcia was the overweight and bumbling assistant to the evil Captain Monasterio of the King's Lancers. Name Garcia's favorite watering hole.

Bonus 1

Q1001. Match the characters with the TV or radio stations on which they worked. Also supply the name of the show and the city or town in which it was set.

1. Bailey Quarters	(A) WKS-TV
2. Frasier Crane	(B) WJM-TV
3. Bobby Soul	(C) AFVN-TV
4. Steven Keaton	(D) KBHR (radio)
5. Matt Cassidy	(E) KGGY-TV
6. Jessica Novak	(F) KXLA-TV
7. Gordie Howard	(G) TAB-TV
8. Ellen Cunningham	(H) KACL (radio)
9. Christine Armstrong	(I) WYN-TV
10. Candi LeRoy	(J) WBN-TV
11. Bill Bittinger	(K) KLA-TV
12. Barth Gimble	(L) WKRP (radio)
13. George Owens	(M) UBS-TV
14. Chris Owens	(N) WBLZ (radio)
15. Tabitha Stephens	(O) WBFL-TV

Zorro

A998. "When you cannot clothe yourself in the skin of a lion put on that of a fox."

A999. A page of sheet music on his father's piano

A1000. The Pasada de Los Angeles

Bonus

A1001. 1 and L ("WKRP in Cincinnati")
2 and H ("Frasier"; Seattle)
3 and N ("Rhythm and Blues"; Detroit)
4 and A ("Family Ties"; Ohio)
5 and I ("Goodnight, Beantown"; Boston)
6 and K ("Jessica Novak"; Los Angeles)
7 and B ("The Mary Tyler Moore Show"; Minneapolis)
8 and G ("W.E.B." New York City)
9 and E ("Coach"; Minneapolis)
10 and C ("The Six O'Clock Follies"; Vietnam)
11 and O ("Buffalo Bill"; Buffalo, N.Y.)
12 and M ("America 2-Night"; Alta Coma, California)
13 and J ("Mr. Belvedere"; Pittsburgh)
14 and D ("Northern Exposure"; Cicely, Alaska)
15 and F ("Tabitha"; Los Angeles)

CHAPTER
4

Cult Shows

Brooklyn Bridge
CBS, 1991–92

Q1002. This nostalgic look at life in Brooklyn in 1956 was seen through the eyes of three generations of a close-knit Jewish family: grandparents Sophie and Jules; their married daughter, Phyllis; her husband, George; and their boys, Alan and Nathaniel. Teenage Alan and friends Benny and Warren hang out oat a local spot call Sid's Candy Store. What is its official name—as seen on the window?

Q1003. Alan and his friends also attend the same school. Name it.

Q1004. A bit of controversy entered the family's lives when Alan began seeing a Catholic girl named Katie Monahan. What school did Katie attend?

Camp Runamuck
NBC, 1965–66

Q1005. "In the middle of farming country" was Camp Runamuck, a sloppily run summer boys' camp owned by Commander Wivenhoe. He was rarely called by a first name, but he did have one. What was it?

Q1006. Across the lake from Runamuck was the girls' camp that Wivenhoe feared (he considered his grounds a paradise free of women). What song did the female campers play at six each morning that drove Wivenhoe batty?

Q1007. At the end of each episode, two bears would comment on the day's activities. What were the bear's names?

Brooklyn Bridge

A1002. Sid Elgart's Fine Confections

A1003. Seth Lowell Junior High

A1004. St. Matthews Grammar School

Camp Runamuck

A1005. Wallace

A1006. "Good Morning to You."

A1007. Irving and Virginia

Diver Dan
Syndicated, 1960

Q1008. The world beneath the sea was home to Diver Dan, a fearless ocean explorer who helped protect the good fish from the evil Baron Barracuda and what dim-witted assistant?

Q1009. Besides such fish as Finley Haddock and Skipper Kipper, Dan also helped the beautiful mermaid that they look to for guidance. Name her.

Q1010. When the mermaid needed to contact Dan, she would use what device to do so?

Doctor Who
Syndicated, 1973

Q1011. The adventures of a Time Lord called Doctor Who and a companion were the focal point of this, the longest running sci-fi series on television (began in England in 1963 and ceased production in 1990). From what planet did our Time Lord hail?

Q1012. The Doctor traveled in a malfunctioning time machine called the TARDIS (it could change its shape, but was stuck in the form of a British police call box). What did TARDIS stand for?

Q1013. The Doctor had a built-in resistance to any form of violence, except for self defense. Name the Time Lord who became a renegade and set out to conquer the universe.

Q1014. In addition to the above enemy, the Doctor had many others (anything that threatened to destroy life). His most treacherous were deadly cone-like robots who spoke in metallic tones. Their most famous words are "Ex-ter-min-ate, ex-ter-min-ate." What were they called?

Q1015. Though he preferred to be called "The Doctor," our Time Lord never had a name (his first traveling companion, Ian, called him Doctor Who). However, in one episode, "Spearhead From Space," the Doctor mentioned his first name. What is it?

Diver Dan

A1008. Trigger Fish

A1009. Minerva

A1010. The Shell-O-Phone

Doctor Who

A1011. Gallifrey

A1012. Time and Relative Dimension in Space

A1013. The Master

A1014. Daleks

A1015. Dr. John Smith

Doctor Who continued

Q1016. Each Time Lord had the ability to regnerate himself twelve times (the reason why seven actors played the Doctor). The First Law of Time prohibited Time Lords from seeing their former and future selves. When the High Command needed to unite Doctors 1, 2, and 3 to battle the evil Omega, though, which Doctor's companion witnessed this forbidden sight?

Q1017. When the Doctor was exiled on Earth he became the scientific adviser to what organization headed by Brigadier Lethbridge-Stewart?

Dracula: The Series
Syndicated, 1990–91

Q1018. Alexander Lucard was a modern-day vampire and the most sophisticated of his breed. He could live in daylight, although he had no vampire powers. What gave Lucard not only his powers, but also his ability to face sunlight?

Q1019. The famous Helsing family of vampire hunters was also represented here by Gustav Helsing. Gustav had seen the movie *The Vampire's Tomb* twenty-seven times and in the 1950s was in what band?

Q1020. Sophie Martineck was a teenager living in Gustav's home while attending school. Alexander was very attracted to Sophie—not only because she was beautiful, but because she possessed his favorite blood type. What was it?

Eerie, Indiana
NBC, 1991–92

Q1021. Normal, Indiana, was the sister city of Eerie, Indiana, "the center of weirdness for the entire planet." All the strange happenings were seen through the eyes of Marshall Teller, a seventh grader who was gathering evidence to prove Eerie was eerie. Each year the citizens celebrated Tornado Day (once a year a tornado hits town). What was the tornado's name?

A1016. Jo Grant

A1017. UNIT—The United Nations Intelligence Task Force

Dracula: The Series

A1018. "A hole in the fabric of time," located behind a secret wall in back of the fireplace in his castle

A1019. The Five Flying Dutchmen and a Dutch Girl

A1020. AB negative

Eerie, Indiana

A1021. Bob

Eerie, Indiana continued

Q1022. The Eerie Dairy provided the town with Eerie Milk ("an udder delight") and the only newspaper was the *Examiner*. What was the name of the town's one department store?

Q1023. Marshall's father, Edgar, was an MIT graduate who worked as a scientist for what company?

Forever Knight
CBS, 1992–95

Q1024. Nick Knight was an 800-year-old bachelor vampire working as a detective for the Toronto Metro Police Department. To get assigned to the night shift, what did Nick tell his captain?

Q1025. Having turned his back on vampirism in 1228, Nick was now pursued by a master vampire named LaCroix. Janette, a beautiful vampire from Nick's past, helped by warning him when LaCroix was near. What nightclub did Janette own?

Q1026. Nick was desperately trying to end his curse by facing his fears. Although tempted to bite the necks of beautiful women, he did not kill for blood. To sustain himself, Nick had a supply of blood from what animal in his refrigerator?

Harry and the Hendersons
Syndicated, 1991–93

Q1027. Fifteen-year-old Sarah Henderson was one day going to write a book about her family—"But I'm going to use a pen name. I don't want anyone to think I'm nuts." In addition to her parents and a brother, Sarah shared her home with Harry, a 680-pound Bigfoot who sort of adopted them as his family. Harry owned a Barry Manilow tape collection and loved granola bars. What did he call granola bars?

A1022. The World o' Stuff

A1023. Things, Inc.

Forever Knight

A1024. That he was allergic to sunlight

A1025. The Raven

A1026. Cow

Harry and the Hendersons

A1027. "Nummie Nummie" or "Num Num"

Harry and the Hendersons continued

Q1028. George, Sarah's father, had a childhood dream to go to Hollywood, meet Annette Funicello, and sing on "The Mickey Mouse Club." After first working for the People's Sporting Goods Company, he then began publishing what magazine?

Q1029. Sarah's mother, Nancy, ate a half-gallon of rocky road ice cream when she got upset, and, according to Nancy, what was the most risqué thing she ever did?

Q1030. The Henderson's neighbor, Samantha Glick, wished they "would get a pet duck like a normal family." She was a television reporter and worked on what show?

M.A.N.T.I.S.
Fox, 1994–95

Q1031. The M.A.N.T.I.S., as he was called, was the secret alias of Dr. Miles Hawkins, a crippled biophysicist who battled crime with the aid of an exo-skeleton (suit) that enabled him to walk. In what city did Miles live?

Q1032. Miles was "just one man trying to help." Assisting him was his friend, Dr. John Stonebreak, who helped Miles devise the M.A.N.T.I.S. Just what did M.A.N.T.I.S. stand for?

Q1033. As M.A.N.T.I.S., Miles wore a black suit (which made him look like a praying mantis) and used paralyzing darts to stop his enemies. Name his base of operations.

Q1034. Also assisting Miles and John were Lt. Leora Maxwell and Taylor Savidge, a courier. For what company did Taylor work?

The Misfits of Science
NBC, 1985–86

Q1035. William Hayes, Elvin Lincoln, Johnny Bukowski, and Gloria Dinallo were four people who possessed extraordinary powers that make them "The Misfits of Science," one of two nicknames for the H.I.T. (Human Investigative Team). By what other nickname were they known?

A1028. *A Better Life*

A1029. "Not to wear a bra between 1972 and 1975."

A1030. "The News at Five"

M.A.N.T.I.S.

A1031. Port Columbia

A1032. Mechanically Augmented Neuro-Transmitter Interception System

A1033. The Seapod

A1034. Iron Horse Couriers

The Misfits of Science

A1035. "Weird Are Us"

The Misfits of Science *continued*

Q1036. Gloria had amazing telekinetic powers and worked as a waitress at the Burger Barn. What was Billy's nickname for her?

Q1037. Johnny was a rock star who was "fried" by 20,000 volts of electricity at his last concert. Now a human dynamo, he was called what by Billy?

My So-Called Life
ABC, 1994–95

Q1038. The heroine of our story is Angela Chase, a pretty fifteen-year-old struggling to cope with friends, family, and first loves. Her father, Graham, thinks everyone in the world is having more fun than he is, and her mother, Betty, runs the family printing business, which she inherited from her father. Name the company.

Q1039. Angela has a rather gloomy outlook on life and a loose cannon of a friend named Rose Ann, who is everything Angela wants to be but can't. What school do they attend?

Q1040. Few things make Angela happy. One is good grades, the other is ice cream. What is her favorite flavor?

Once a Hero
ABC, 1987

Q1041. Pleasantville was a city created by Abner Bevis for comic book hero Captain Justice to protect. When not avenging crime, Captain Justice was someone else. Who was he?

Q1042. Captain Justice wore a red outfit with blue gloves and a blue triangle on his chest with a gold C.J. in the center. By what other name was Captain Justice known?

Q1043. When Captain Justice crossed the Forbidden Zone to go to the real world, the Great and Magnificent One, ruler of the Comic Book World, sent someone to return him to his own World. Who was assigned this mission?

A1036. "Glo"

A1037. "B-Man"

My So-Called Life

A1038. The Wood Printing Company

A1039. Liberty High

A1040 Cookie dough

Once a Hero

A1041. Brad Steele

A1042. The Crimson Crusader

A1043. Gumshoe, a 1940s-style detective

seaQuest, DSV
NBC, 1993–

Q1044. It is twenty-five years into the future and the last frontier is being explored: the sea via the *seaQuest*, a Nautilus-like submarine commanded by Capt. Nathan Bridger. For what part of the government does the *seaQuest* work?

Q1045. Once the oceans are explored and peace is established, what is to become of the *seaQuest*?

Q1046. The *seaQuest* is 1,000 feet long, carries 312 people (88 military, 224 scientists), but what does DSV stand for?

Q1047. Although the *seaQuest* roams the seven seas, it does have a home base. Where is it?

The Super Human Samurai Syber Squad
Syndicated, 1994

Q1048. Sam Collins was a high school student who, along with friends Sydney, Amp, and Tank, battled Kilokahn, the overlord of the digital world. Kilokahn lived inside computer circuits and created mega monsters to attack electronic systems. Who helped Kilokahn create the monsters?

Q1049. The four Syber Squad pals attended North Valley High School and had a rock band. What was its name?

Q1050. When helping Sam in the computer world, Sydney, Amp, and Tank had body armor ships. Amp's was Vitor. Name either Sydney's or Tank's ship.

Thunder in Paradise
Syndicated, 1994–95

Q1051. R. J. Spencer and Martin Brubaker are ex-Navy Seals who own Thunder, a high tech boat for hire. How much a day does it cost to hire Thunder?

seaQuest, DSV

A1044. The UEO (United Earth Organization)

A1045. It will become a research vessel

A1046. Deep Submergence Vehicle

A1047. Pearl Harbor, Hawaii

The Super Human Samurai Syber Squad

A1048. Malcolm Frink

A1049. Team Samurai

A1050. Sydney's was Vor; Tank's was Trackton

Thunder in Paradise

A1051. $5,000

Thunder in Paradise continued

Q1052. Their friend, Kelly LaRue, is a former model who now owns the local beach watering hole. Name it.

Q1053. Thunder is capable of fantastic speeds and has advanced technology, a voice-responsive computer, and an array of weapons. Spencer, who designed Thunder, is hoping to take it to what next step of development?

A1052. The Scuttlebutt Bar

A1053. Sub oceanic

CHAPTER
5

Limited Run Series

Titles listed fall into the assorted categories of pilot series, limited runs, trial series, test series, and spring and summer shows. Such shows are usually limited to between four and eight episodes, but if they prove successful on their tryouts, they are usually picked up for regular season runs (*Three's Company*, *Cagney and Lacey*, and *Ellen* are such limited runs that went on to became hits).

Bill and Ted's Excellent Adventures
Fox, 1992

Q1054. In the year 2692, the people of San Demas, California, live in a society based on the philosophy of Bill and Ted, called "The Two Great Ones," and the music of their band. Name their band.

Q1055. In this "most excellent world," the Holy One rules and one man has been assigned to protect Bill and Ted. Who is he?

Q1056. When Bill and Ted are not playing with their band, they work as salesmen in what store managed by Mr. Kerlson?

Blansky's Beauties
ABC, 1977

Q1057. Nancy Blansky was a Las Vegas show producer and the den mother to a group of budding showgirls called Blansky's Beauties. At what hotel did she work?

Q1058. Pat Morita played Arnold Takahashi, the owner of Arnold's Coffee Shop. The character first appeared on *Happy Days* as the owner of Arnold's Drive-In. Nancy also had ties to that show. She was the cousin of which character?

Bill and Ted's Excellent Adventures

A1054. The Wyld Stallyns

A1055. Rufus

A1056 Nail World

Blanşky's Beauties

A1057 The Oasis

A1058 Howard Cunningham

Broken Badges
CBS, 1992

Q1059. A "broken badge" referred to a cop on psychiatric leave. Beau Jack Bowman was a sergeant who had been assigned three such cops: Judy, Stanley, and Toby. What did Bowman call his team?

Q1060. Punk-pretty, Rambo-style motorcycle cop Judy loved to wear leather and revealing blouses. However "I don't like guys starring at my chest, it makes me angry." Why did you not want to get Judy angry?

Q1061. Stanley was a street cop for three years before pressure caused him to retreat to a ventriloquist's world. He then communicated through his dummy. Name his wooden buddy.

Q1062. Toby suffered from fits of depression and deep self-hatred. When situations became stressful, he believed he was an Old West Texas Ranger. What was the ranger named?

Delta House
ABC, 1979

Q1063. This series is based on the feature film *Animal House* and relates the antics of the students of the Delta House fraternity at Faber College. These students, called "Animals," are a disgrace to the campus and shun the philosophy of the school's founder, Emil Faber. What was his philosophy?

Q1064. The legacy of Delta House is "to hang out with a bunch of animals and get drunk every weekend." They have a proud tradition ("Don't get mad, get even") and a secret weapon. What is their secret weapon?

Broken Badges

A1059. The Cobra Squad

A1060. " 'Cause I'm a street bitch with an attitude."

A1061. Officer Danny

A1062. Cactus Cole Watson

Delta House

A1063. "Knowledge is Good."

A1064. A stunning blonde they call "Bombshell."

Code Name: Foxfire
NBC, 1985

Q1065. Liz Towne is a beautiful CIA agent (code name: Foxfire) who was framed for smuggling counterfeit pesos into Mexico. The government knew she was innocent, but clearing her would cost the lives of a dozen people. As a result, Liz was sent to prison. How long a term did she serve?

Q1066. Liz now works for Larry Hutchins, the brother of the President of the United States. Larry is publicly thought of as a fool (his cover is that of "a national bozo") and shares the same security level as Liz. What is it?

Double Rush
CBS, 1995

Q1067. Johnny Verona owns a Manhattan messenger service called Double Rush. A rush message is delivered within forty-five minutes by bicycle; if you order a double rush, how long will it take you to get your package?

Q1068. Hunter, Leo, Zoey, and the Kid, an old-timer, are some of the couriers who work for Johnny. Hunter is the fastest messenger Johnny has. He's so fast, what can he beat, according to Johnny?

Q1069. Zoey is the only girl employed at Double Rush. She took the job because she couldn't find work anyplace else. From what university did Zoey graduate?

Q1070 Johnny's dream was to become a rock star, but it never came true. When he was younger he worked for the rival Ed Foley Couriers so he could buy something he saw and desperately wanted. What was it?

Code Name: Foxfire

A1065. 1,560 days

A1066. G-36

Double Rush

A1067. Twenty minutes

A1068. A fax machine

A1069   Harvard Business School

A1070. a used Jimi Hendrix guitar

Fast Times
CBS, 1986

Q1071. This television version of *Fast Times at Ridemont High* continued to follow events in the lives of students Linda Barrett and Stacey Hamilton. In the 1982 film, the girls worked at the Bronco Burger; what was it called in the series?

Q1072. Mr. Hand was the stern history teacher who locked his classroom door when the third bell sounds. He never laughed in class; when he felt like a laugh what did he do?

Fish Police
CBS, 1992

Q1073. "I'm a cop who's a carp" said Inspector Gil, who was based in Fish City, a polluted, crime-ridden ocean city. Fort Lox was the treasury and Haddica its prison. What was the name of the local newspaper?

Q1074. The Shell Shack was the local watering hole where Angel, called "Chick of the Sea," was the sexy singer who once worked for Gil as his "fish Friday." What did Gil call Angel's breasts—and for extra points, what brand of bra did Angela wear?

Q1075. Gil frequented Pearl's Diner, and Pearl, the owner, named a special after him called the Inspector Gil. If you ordered this dish, what would you get?

Get Smart
Fox, 1995

Q1076. In this update of the 1960s series of the same title, Maxwell Smart now headed CONTROL, and his wife, 99, was a congresswoman. Their son, Zack, was a CONTROL agent and his partner was the beautiful if snobbish Agent 66 (like 99, she had no other name). KAOS, which still plagued Max, had a new plan to take over the world. What was it?

Fast Times

A1071. Cattle Burger

A1072. He goes home and reads his students' test papers

Fish Police

A1073. The *Ancient Mariner*

A1074. Her breasts are "Those Babies"; she wears a Maidenform Bra.

A1075. Corn flakes and coffee

Get Smart

A1076. Total World Economic Domination

Get Smart *continued*

Q1077. Klutzy Zack was as bumbling as his father and sported sneaker phones (Max, of course, had the shoe phone). Agent 66 knew she was beautiful and could manipulate men ("I do it everyday"). Where did she carry her phone, which also doubled as a gun?

Q1078. Agent 99 was the only level-headed member of the family—well, most of the time. Why didn't she liked to be called Mrs. Smart?

High Sierra Search and Rescue
NBC, 1995

Q1079. Tooter Campbell is the head of a group of volunteers who risk their lives to help people trapped in perilous situations. Name the group Tooter heads.

Q1080. Tooter got his nickname from playing the bagpipes and earns a living as a helicopter pilot. He also has a favorite watering hole. Name it.

Mann and Machine
NBC, 1992

Q1081. Sgt. Eve Edison and her partner, Detective Bobby Mann, were with the L.A.P.D. of "the near future." When Bobby's partner, Warner, a bucket of bolts lab-created robot, was put out of commission by a bullet, he teamed with Eve, a beautiful female robot programmed to be the perfect cop. Eve represented a new breed of cop called what?

Q1082. Although highly advanced in technical (and physical) terms, emotionally Eve was quite young—the age of a seven-year-old. She learned a lot from watching TV and she had a lucky number. What was it?

Q1083. Eve had to experience the good and bad part of life. Although made of plastic and metal, she could eat and drink but could "squeak" if she got rusty. No, she didn't carry an oil can (like the Tin Man in *The Wizard of Oz*). What prevented Eve from rusting?

A1077. Her Phone Bra or Bullet Bra

A1078. "That makes me feel like 100. Call me 99."

High Sierra Search and Rescue

A1079. Bear Valley Search and Rescue

A1080. The Red Dog Saloon

Mann and Machine

A1081. The Protector

A1082. The algebra term pi

A1083. The tears in her eyes, which are a lubricant

On the Air
ABC, 1992

Q1084. The problems faced by talent and crew attempting to put on a live TV show in the 1950s was the focus of this series. Here it was *The Lester Guy Show*. On what fictional network did it air?

Q1085. Blinky Watts was the show's assistant sound effects man and suffered from Bozman Symplex. What was this ailment?

Q1086. What dog food company sponsored *The Lester Guy Show*?

Sydney
CBS, 1990

Q1087. Sydney Kells, played by Valerie Bertinelli, was a 25-year-old single woman who worked as an investigator for what law firm?

Q1088. Chocolate milk was Sydney's favorite drink. She first cried when Dick Sargent replaced Dick York on *Bewitched* and had a cat named Calvin. She also had a rather unusual favorite sandwich. What was it?

Q1089. Private eye Sydney's best friend Jill was a fashion model for what company?

Q1090. Jill liked to lounge around the house in a bathrobe and shared her first secret with Sydney when she was twelve. Who did Jill tell Sydney her hero was?

On the Air

A1084. ZBC (Zoblotnick Broadcasting Corporation)

A1085. "He appears to be blind but isn't. Blinky sees 25.6 times as much as we do."

A1086. Wembley Snaps

Sydney

A1087. Fenton, Benton and Sloane

A1088. Hershey bars with almonds on white bread

A1089. Contemporary Fashions

A1090. Mighty Mouse

Vinnie and Bobby
Fox, 1992

Q1091. Vinnie Verducci and his best friend, Bobby Grazzo, shared an apartment and were construction workers for what company?

Q1092. Vinnie's neighbor, the ultra sexy Mona Mullins, couldn't wait until she was eighteen so she could marry him. However Vinnie had no interest in a seventeen-year-old girl whose father owned a gun shop. When Vinnie upset Mona by turning down her advances, what did Mona do to cool off?

Q1093. Bobby was most concerned with his hair and used the world's most powerful hair dryer. What was it called?

Q1094. When Bobby flexed his muscles, it turned Mona off. When Vinnie flexed his, Mona was all aglow. What did Vinnie call his muscles?

Vinnie and Bobby

A1091. Rand Construction

A1092. She decapitates her Ken dolls

A1093. The Omni Magnum 2000

A1094. Thunder and Lightning

6

Who Replaced Whom?

The following questions refer to cast replacements, the best known example being Dick Sargent replacing Dick York as Darrin on *Bewitched*.

The A-Team
NBC, 1983–87

Q1095. Templeton Peck, better known as Face, was a great con artist who helped the team get what they needed without paying for it. However, Dirk Benedict was not originally cast as Face. Who was the original Face (replaced because he looked too young to be a Vietnam vet)?

Bachelor Father
CBS, NBC, ABC, 1957–62

Q1096. Suave and sophisticated bachelor attorney Bentley Gregg began the series with a secretary named Vickie (played by Alice Backes) and ended with one named Connie (Sally Mansfield). Two additional secretaries appeared, one after Vickie and one before Connie. Name either one.

Batman
ABC, 1966–68

Q1097. Gotham City was plagued by numerous villains whom Batman and Robin could never really seem to defeat. Sexy but dangerous Catwoman purred her way into Batman's heart and was played initially by Julie Newmar. Lee Meriwether had the part in the 1966 theatrical film *Batman*, but what actress took over the TV role?

Who Replaced Whom?

A1095. Tim Dunigan

A1096. Kitty Devereaux, played first by Shirley Mitchell and then by Jane Nigh; then Kitty Marsh, played by Sue Ane Langdon

A1097. Eartha Kitt

Batman *continued*

Q1098. Another criminal who parried with Batman was the cold-hearted Mr. Freeze. George Sanders originated the role, but who replaced him?

Q1099. This third Batman foe left behind clues that rhymed but made no sense. It took the keen minds of Batman and Robin to decipher the words of the fun-loving Riddler, a role begun by Frank Gorshin. Who replaced him?

Baywatch
Syndicated, 1991

Q1100. When lifeguard Summer Quinn (played by Nicole Eggert) decided to return home to Philadelphia to attend college, she was replaced by an equally gorgeous lifeguard played by Yasmine Bleeth. What is the character's name?

Bewitched
ABC, 1964–72

Q1101. In addition to Dick Sargent replacing Dick York, there was also a replacement for Louise Tate, wife of Darrin's boss, Larry. Irene Vernon first played the role. Who replaced her?

Big Town
1950–56

Q1102. Patrick McVey was TV's first Steve Wilson, a newspaper reporter for the *Illustrated Press*. Lorelie Kilbourne was his assistant. Who played the second Steve Wilson?

Q1103. *Big Town* ran for only six years and six actresses played Lorelei Kilbourne. Margaret Hayes was the first and Julie Stevens the last. Name any of the other four actresses in the role.

A1098. Eli Wallach first, then Otto Preminger

A1099. John Astin

A1100. Caroline Holden

A1101. Kasey Rogers

A1102. Mark Stevens

A1103. Jane Nigh, Beverly Tyler, Trudy Wroe, Mary K. Wells

The Brady Bunch
ABC, 1969–74

Q1104. Throughout the long run of this series under various titles (also *The Brady Kids, The Brady Brides, The Brady Bunch Hour,* and *The Bradys*), only two of the children (Marcia and Jan) were replaced at one time or another. Maureen McCormick began the role of Marcia, but in *The Bradys* (CBS, 1990), she was replaced by what actress?

Q1105. Eve Plumb originated the role of Jan Brady, dropped out for *The Brady Bunch Hour* (ABC, 1977), but returned to the role for the other versions. Who played Jan in 1977?

Buck Rogers in the Twenty-Fifth Century
NBC, 1979–81

Q1106. Princess Ardella, ruler of the planet Draconia, sought to marry Buck, but never realized her dream. She was assisted by the evil Kane, a part made famous ultimately by Michael Ansara. But who originated the role here?

Cover Up
CBS, 1984–85

Q1107. Dani Reynolds (Jennifer O'Neill) was a photographer who was actually an espionage agent for the government. She was first assisted by Jon-Erik Hexum as Mac Harper, who posed as her model. When Hexum accidentally shot himself he was replaced by Antony Hamilton as what character?

Dr. Quinn, Medicine Woman
CBS, 1993–

Q1108. It was a very subtle change and no attention was brought to it. But if you're a fan of the show you may have noticed that Dr. Quinn's eldest ward, Colleen, is no longer being played by Erika Flores. Who is now playing Colleen?

A1104. Leah Ayres

A1105. Geri Reschel

A1106. Henry Silva

A1107. Jack Stryker

A1108. Jessica Bowman

Empty Nest
NBC, 1988–95

Q1109. When Kristy McNichol became ill several seasons into the show's run and her character, Barbara, had to be replaced, Harry's never-before-seen daughter, Emily, was brought on. Who played Emily?

Gilligan's Island
CBS, 1964–67

Q1110. Even if you have never seen the program you somehow know that Tina Louise played curvaceous movie star Ginger Grant. However, when three TV movies were made in 1978 (*Rescue From Gilligan's Island*), 1979 (*The Castaways on Gilligan's Island*), and 1981 (*The Harlem Globetrotters on Gilligan's Island*), two actresses replaced Tina as Ginger. Constance Forslund was Ginger in the third film, but who played the part in the first two?

Happy Days
ABC, 1974–84

Q1111. Life in Milwaukee during the 1950s was seen through the eyes of the Cunningham family—parents Howard and Marion and their children Richie, Joanie, and Chuck. Chuck? Yes, he was there and three actors played him. Name any one.

Home Improvement
ABC, 1991–

Q1112. Besides Tim "The Tool Man" Taylor and his helper Al Borland, the TV show *Tool Time* has one other regular— the gorgeous girl who assists them. She is now played by Debbie Dunning as Debbie. Who played her, as Lisa, during the first season?

A1109 Lisa Rieffel

A1110. Judith Baldwin

A1111. Ric Carrott, Gavan O'Herlihy, Randolph Roberts

A1112. Pamela Anderson (now of *Baywatch*)

How to Marry a Millionaire
Syndicated, 1958–60

Ql l l3. The adventures of three beautiful girls trying to land millionaire husbands was depicted through the experiences of Loco, Mike, and Greta. In second season episodes, Greta, played by Lori Nelson, left to get married. Lisa Gaye became the new girl on the team. What character did she play?

Timmy and Lassie
CBS, 1957–64

Ql l l4. It is well known that Jon Provost (Timmy) replaced Tommy Rettig (Jeff) and that June Lockhart and Hugh Reilly played Timmy's parents, Ruth and Paul Martin. June and Hugh were also replacements. Who originally played Ruth and Paul Martin?

Little House on the Prairie
NBC, 1974–82

Ql l l5. Even animal "actors" get replaced. Laura's best friend on the show was her dog, Jack. Name the dog that replaced him?

Make Room for Daddy
ABC, CBS, 1953–64.

Ql l l6. Nightclub comedian Danny Williams and his wife, Margaret, had two children, Terry and Rusty. Sherry Jackson originated the role of Terry, but when the series moved from ABC to CBS in 1957, Danny married Kathy (a widow with a daughter named Linda) and a new actress played Terry. Who was she?

Martin Kane, Private Eye
NBC, 1949–54

Ql l l7. Martin Kane was a hard-boiled detective who achieved results through determination and force of character. He was played first by William Gargan, then by Lloyd Nolan. Who followed Nolan in the role?

A1113. Gwen Laurel

A1114. Cloris Leachman and Jon Shepodd

A1115. Bandit

A1116. Penny Parker

A1117. Lee Tracy, then Mark Stevens

The Mary Tyler Moore Show
CBS, 1970–77

Q1118. One of the most unforgetable characters to appear on the show was Chuckles the Clown, a star of his own program on WJM-TV who met an unfortunate end—dressed as a peanut for a parade, he was killed by an elephant who tried to shell him. Name either of the two actors who played Chuckles.

M*A*S*H
CBS, 1972–82

Q1119. There were a number of changes on the show over the years including Harry Morgan replacing McLean Stevenson and Mike Farrell replacing Wayne Rogers. William Christopher is the actor known for playing the chaplain, Father Francis Mulcahy. But who originated the role in the pilot episode?

Maude
CBS, 1972–78

Q1120. Maude, the outspoken liberal, had a voluptuous daughter named Carol, played by Adrienne Barbeau. However, on *All in the Family*, the show from which *Maude* was spun-off, Maude's daughter was not as glamorous or as busty as Adrienne's Carol. Who was the original Carol?

The Mothers-in-Law
NBC, 1967–69

Q1121. Kaye and Roger Buell were the neighbors of Eve and Herb Hubbard. Roger was a free-lance TV writer and was first played by Roger C. Carmel. Who played the part in second season episodes?

A1118. Mark Gordon or Richard Schaal

A1119 George Morgan

A1120. Marcia Rodd

A1121 Richard Deacon

The Munsters
CBS, 1964–66

Q1122. That creepy family living at 1313 Mockingbird Lane was resurrected on TV from 1988 to 1991 when *The Munsters Today* appeared in syndication. The same characters were back but played by different people. John Schuck had the Fred Gwynne role of Herman Munster and Lee Meriwether took over the Yvonne DeCarlo part of Lily. In the original series, first Beverley Owen and then Pat Priest played Marilyn. Who played Marilyn in the new version?

Nancy Drew
ABC, 1977

Q1123. Teenage sleuth Nancy Drew, the daughter of attorney Carson Drew, was originally played by Pamela Sue Martin. Who succeeded her in the part?

The Partridge Family
ABC, 1970–74

Q1124. It is common knowledge among trivia buffs that Brian Forster replaced Jeremy Gelbwalks as Chris Partridge, but there was also one other replacement on the series, that of Shirley Partridge's father, Walter Renfrew. Ray Bolger originated the role. Who replaced him?

Petticoat Junction
CBS, 1963–70

Q1125. Jeannine Riley, Pat Woodell, and Linda Kaye Henning played Billie Jo, Bobbie Jo, and Betty Jo, the daughters of Kate Bradley, owner of the Shady Rest Hotel. Who were the second actresses to play Billie Jo and Bobbie Jo?

A1122 Hilary Van Dyke

A1123. Janet Louise Johnson (a.k.a. Janet Julian)

A1124. Jackie Coogan

A1125. Gunilla Hutton as Billie Jo; Lori Saunders as Bobbie Jo

Saved by the Bell: The College Years
NBC, 1993–94

Q1126. When the original *Saved by the Bell* teenagers graduated from high school and went off to college, Zack, Screech, and Slater were seen at California University. They shared a dorm room with three girls (Leslie, Alex, and Danielle). The stunning Kelly Kapowski from the original series was brought back shortly after the premiere to boost sagging ratings and become a love interest for Zack. Which girl did Kelly replace?

77 Sunset Strip
ABC, 1958–63

Q1127. Gerald Lloyd Kookson III, better known as Kookie, was the parking lot attendant at Dino's, the nightclub next to 77 Sunset Strip. When Kookie was "promoted" to private eye, who replaced him as the car parker and what was his character name?

Three's Company
ABC, 1977–84

Q1128. Jack, Janet, and Chrissy are best known as the roommates who shared Apartment 201 at the Ropers. But before Jack, Janet and Chrissy had another female roommate who left to get married. Whom did Jack replace?

Topper
CBS, 1953–55

Q1129. It appeared that working for Cosmo Topper, a man haunted by the ghosts of George and Marian Kerby and their dog Neil, proved too much for Katie, the maid (played by Kathleen Freeman), who left after the first season. Edna Skinner was brought on to replace her as the new maid. What was her name?

A1126. Danielle

A1127. Robert Logan as J.R. Hale

A1128. Eleanor Garvey, played by Marianne Black

A1129. Maggie.

7

TV Themes

A series theme song or opening narration is sometimes better remembered than the show itself. You won't find here the all too familiar "Just sit right back and you'll hear a tale..." or "Come listen to my story about a man named Jed..." What you will find is a selection of theme excerpts from many well known as well as lesser shows from the fifties through the mind-nineties. A blank within a theme indicates the name of the show; the first thirteen questions are words spoken by an announcer.

Q1130. "Whenever the laws of any state are broken, a duly authorized organization swings into action. It may be called the state police, state troopers, militia, the Rangers, or the Highway Patrol. These are the stories of the men whose training, skill, and courage have enforced and preserved our state laws."

Q1131. "Space Academy in the world beyond tomorrow. Here the Space Cadets train for duty on distant planets. In roaring rockets they blast through the millions of miles from Earth to far-flung stars and brave the dangers of cosmic frontiers, protecting the liberties of the planets, safeguarding the cause of universal peace in the age of the conquest of space."

Q1132. "This is Buddy Overstreet. He's wanted by the head of the most powerful crime syndicate in the country. In a steamroom Buddy overheard their vital secrets and the mysterious words Chicken Little. Now he knows too much. These are the orders given to all members of the syndicate from one end of the country to the other—'Get him, get him, get him.'"

TV Themes

A1130. *Highway Patrol* (1956)

A1131. *Tom Corbett, Space Cadet* (1950)

A1132. *Run, Buddy, Run* (1966)

QI 133. "Peter Murphy, American secret agent marked for death meets a bizarre destiny. As his pursuers close in he comes face to face with his exact double, multi-millionaire Mark Wainwright. The millionaire takes the bullet meant for the spy and Murphy finds the perfect cover. He steps into the shoes and life of the man with his face, and Peter Murphy becomes _____."

QI 134. "Nothing travels faster than news. An electronic impulse splinters distance at 186,000 miles a second. From Tokyo, from London, from Rio, from New York. An age of speed and curiosity. The news probes and the probe is truth."

QI 135. "Democracy is a very bad form of government but I ask you never to forget it; all the others are so much worse."

QI 136. "There is nothing wrong with your television set, do not attempt to adjust the picture....For the next hour sit quietly and we will control all that you see and hear. You are about to participate in a great adventure; you are about to experience the awe and mystery which reaches from the inner mind to _____."

QI 137. "Whatever it is, wherever it is, at home or around the world, you see it here. _____, and here's your host, Jack Smith."

QI 138. "...He journied the earth battling his wicked step-mother, Hera, the all-powerful queen of the gods. But wherever there was evil, wherever an innocent would suffer, there would be_____."

QI 139. "Up, up, rockets blazing with white hot fury, the man-made meteors ride through the atmosphere, breaking the gravity barrier, pushing up and out, faster and faster then outer space for _____."

A1133. *The Man Who Never Was* (1966)

A1134. *Wire Service* (1956)

A1135. *Slattery's People* (1964)

A1136. *The Outer Limits* (1963)

A1137. *You Asked for It* (1950)

A1138. *Hercules: The Legendary Journeys* (1995)

A1139. *Rod Brown of the Rocket Rangers* (1953)

Q1140. "From Hollywood, the glamour capital of the world, join us in a make-believe search for the most beautiful girl on earth…and although this is not a real contest, we will bring you our version of the all-American beauty. The one-of-a-kind girl who not only has personality and poise, but beauty and talent as well…and now, here's your host and star of the show, Mr. Beauty himself, Rip Taylor."

Q1141. "High adventure in the wild vast regions of outer space. Missions of daring in the name of interplanetary justice. Travel into the future with Buzz Corey, commander-in-chief of the _____."

Q1142. "I am _____ and I know many tales hidden in the hearts of men and women who have stepped into the shadows. Yes, I know the nameless terrors of which they dare not speak."

Q1143. "I'll tell you a story, a real true life story, a tale of the western frontier; the West it was lawless, but one man was flawless and his is the story you'll hear."

Q1144. "Take me back so I can see the way it was my legacy. I need to find what once was good in traces of my childhood."

Q1145. "We've got a gorilla for sale…won't you buy him, take him home and try him…see in the window…full of charm and appeal, handsome, elegant, intelligent, sweet, he's really ideal."

Q1146. "I wish I was a spaceman, the fastest guy alive, I'd fly you 'round the universe in _____. Way out in space together, conquerers of the sky."

Q1147. "…wants a gal who's dreamy…wants a gal who's creamy…wants a gal to call his own."

Q1148. "With beauty and grace as swift as can be, watch it flying through the air…it travels in space or under the sea and it can journey anywhere."

Q1149. "Whistle me up a memory, whistle me back where I wanna be, whistle me a tune that'll carry me to _____."

A1140. *The $1.98 Beauty Show* (1978)

A1141. *Space Patrol* (1950)

A1142. *The Whistler* (1954)

A1143. *The Life and Legend of Wyatt Earp* (1955)

A1144. *The Family Holvak* (1975)

A1145. *The Magilla Gorilla Show* (1964)

A1146. *Fireball XL-5* (1963)

A1147. *Dobie Gillis* (1959)

A1148. *Supercar* (1962)

A1149. *Tombstone Territory* (1957)

Q1150. "Lady Godiva was a freedom rider, she didn't care if the whole world looked....Isadora was the first bra burner...and when the country was fallin' apart, Betsy Ross got it all sewed up. And then there's _____, that uncompromising, enterprising, anything but tranquilizing, right on _____."

Q1151. "I've traveled here, I've traveled there, I guess I've been most everywhere, but I like where I am today and here is where I'll stay."

Q1152. "Marina, I want Marina, what are these strange enchantments that start whenever you're near? Marina, I want Marina, why can't you whisper the words that my heart is longing to hear?"

Q1153. "...and so I go my lonely way, every day filled with danger, even to myself a stranger, wondering who am I."

Q1154. "They've got the fever, got the fever, gold fever. Got the fever, got the fever, gold, gold, gold..."

Q1155. "Katie, all the fellas fall for Katie, 'cause Katie is the gal they adore."

Q1156. "He's the greatest man we know, say he's not and you'll be walking the plank, sir....Let's go a roaming, a roaming across the ocean, let's go a roaming and join _____."

Q1157. "From the coonskin cap on the top of ol' Dan to the heel of his rawhide shoe, the rippenist, roarinist, fightinest man the frontier ever knew."

Q1158. "Who lives down in deepest, darkest Africa? Who's the one who brought the jungle fame? Who's the king of animals in Africa? _____ is his name."

Q1159. "In our little house there's dad and mother...sister and brother and sometimes there is another sister or brother. In our little house there's always _____."

Q1160. "...no one you see is smarter than he, and we know _____ lives in a world full of wonder, lying there under, under the sea."

A1150. *Maude* (1972)

A1151. *The Californians* (1957)

A1152. *Stingray* (1965)

A1153. *Coronet Blue* (1967)

A1154. *The Alaskans* (1959)

A1155. *The Ann Sothern Show* (1958)

A1156. *The Buccaneers* (1956)

A1157. *Daniel Boone* (1964)

A1158. *Kimba, the White Lion* (1966)

A1159. *Room for One More* (1962)

A1160. *Flipper* (1964)

Q1161. "Dream away little man, dream as long as you can, don't grow up I beg of you. Dreams are made for children and we're children as long as we can dream."

Q1162. "All the world is waiting for you and the powers you possess; in your satin tights, fighting for your rights and the old red, white and blue...."

Q1163. "He was innocent, not a charge was true, but the world would never know. _____ scorned as the one who ran, what do you do when you're _____ and you know you're a man?"

Q1164. "She's my very own guiding star, a 1928 Porter, that's my mother dear, she helps me through everything I do and I'm so glad she's here...."

Q1165. "We're just trying to be friendly, come and watch us sing and play, we're the young generation and we've got something to say."

Q1166. "No phone, no lights, no motorcars, not a single luxury, like Robinson Crusoe, it's primitive as can be..."

Q1167. "A man who rides all alone and all that he'll ever own is just a badge and a gun, and he's known as the _____."

Q1168. "Rain and wind and weather, hell bent for leather, wishin' my gal was by my side. All the things I'm missin' could be this love and kissin' are waitin' at the end of my ride..."

Q1169. "Jammin' gears has got to be a fever, a lot of men become addicted to the grind; it takes a special breed to be a truck drivin' man and a steady hand to haul the load behind."

Q1170. "On your mark, get set and go now, got a dream and we just know now, we're gonna make that dream come true— and we'll do it our way, yes, our way...make all of our dreams come true for me and you."

Q1171. "He's my man, ah, he's the man, yeah, let me tell ya about him, can't do without him, just one of a kind, now he's the man, the _____."

A1161. *Shirley Temple's Storybook* (1958)

A1162. *Wonder Woman* (1976)

A1163. *Branded* (1965)

A1164. *My Mother, the Car* (1965)

A1165. *The Monkees* (1966)

A1166. *Gilligan's Island* (1964; the closing theme)

A1167. *Lawman* (1958)

A1168. *Rawhide* (1959)

A1169. *Movin' On* (1974)

A1170. *Laverne and Shirley* (1976)

A1171. *The Six Million Dollar Man* (1973)

Q1172. "There was a gun that won the West, there was a man among the rest, the fastest gun or man alive, a lightning bolt when he drew that _____."

Q1173. "Like a streak of lightning flashing across the sky; like the swiftest arrow whizzing from a bow; like a mighty cannonball he seems to fly."

Q1174. "From San Antone to the Rio Grande, on mountain peaks or desert sand, every outlaw feared the hand of danger, this Texas Ranger."

Q1175. "We all had an uncle and his name was Sam, we had to go in and get him out of a jam; the job wasn't easy, but the burden was shared, back in the forties when everyone cared."

Q1176. "I'm standing on the edge of tomorrow and it's all up to me how far I go...I'm standing on the edge of tomorrow today."

Q1177. "Come and listen to my story, yes, listen while I sing of days of old in England when Arthur was the king..."

Q1178. "He'll dry clean your clothes, be a butler or a porter if it means another quarter in the bank. He'll get his degree, his Phi Beta key—and get them both for free, that's _____."

Q1179. "The trail that he blazed is still there, no one has come since to replace his name, and those with too ready a trigger forgot to figure on his marching cane."

Q1180. "People let me tell you about my best friend, he's a warm-hearted person who'll love me till the end...He's a one boy cuddly toy, my up, my down, my pride and joy."

Q1181. "There's a new girl in town with a brand new style, she was just passing through but if things work out, she's gonna stay awhile."

Q1182. "Girls, girls, girls, don't you wanna love 'em...some made of sugar, some made of spice, all made of everything that's nice, girls, girls, girls."

A1172. *Colt .45* (1957)

A1173. *The Adventures of Champion* (the Wonder Horse; 1955)

A1174. *Rango* (1967)

A1175. *The Goodtime Girls* (1980)

A1176. *Saved by the Bell: The College Years* (1993)

A1177. *The Adventures of Sir Lancelot* (1956)

A1178. *Hank* (1965)

A1179. *Bat Masterson* (1958)

A1180. *The Courtship of Eddie's Father* (1969)

A1181. *Alice* (1976)

A1182. *Sugartime* (1977)

Q1183. "Got tired of packing and unpacking, town to town, up and down the dial, Maybe you and me were never meant to be, just maybe think of me once in awhile, I'm at _____."

Q1184. "Just the good old boys, wouldn't change if they could, fightin' the system like two modern day Robin Hoods."

Q1185. "Rollin' down to Dallas, my wheels provide my palace; off to New Orleans or who knows where, places new and ladies too, I'm B. J. McKay and this is my best friend Bear."

Q1186. "She's mine alone but luckily for you, if you find a girl to love, only one girl to love, then she'll be _____ too."

Q1187. "You're doomed to wander on beyond this land so lonely...so roam in search of home 'cross this land so lonely."

Q1188. "Stop, look, listen 'cause you're gonna hear a brand new story 'bout a brave engineer, he's the greatest of them all we claim, number one's his engine, _____ his name."

Q1189. "There's a man who leads a life of danger and everyone he meets he stays a stranger. With every move he makes, another chance he takes, odds are he won't live to see tomorrow."

Q1190. "Riverboat ring your bell, fare-the-well Annabelle, luck is the lady that he loves the best. Natchez to New Orleans, livin' on jacks and queens, _____ is the legend of the west."

Q1191. "He was cursed with a quick and restless gun and he played the game that no man every won; but his killing turned him cold, he grew bitter, he grew bold and he fought the world with a code of hungry guns..."

Q1192. "This is it, the night of nights; no more rehearsing and nursing a part, we know every part by heart."

Q1193. "Sundance, Sundance, anywhere you wander, my heart's riding with you. Sundance, Sundance, just beyond the sunset love is waitin' for you."

A1183. *WKRP in Cincinnati* (1978)

A1184. *The Dukes of Hazzard* (1979)

A1185. *B. J. and the Bear* (1979)

A1186. *That Girl* (1966)

A1187. *A Man Called Shenandoah* (1965)

A1188. *Casey Jones* (1957)

A1189. *Secret Agent* (1965)

A1190. *Maverick* (1957)

A1191. *The Legend of Jesse James* (1965)

A1192. *The Bugs Bunny Show* (1975)

A1193. *Hotel De Paree* (1959)

Q1194. "See them all, racketeers and their gun molls, fun molls. Prohibition and bathtub gin, if Benny sent you, you walk right into a speakeasy, speak easy. Come along to the song of _____."

Q1195. "A foreign spy arrives by the name of U-31; on his first day in he's done in by a hit-and-run. Got to find a man with the same face as 31. But who?

Q1196. "Saddle up, saddle up, saddle up. This is the story of _____ who rode the Arizona Territory...Praise be the glory of _____ whose courage helped to build the territory. Ride on, ride on, ride on."

Q1197. "If you only had a penny to your name, you'd go and buy her a bright and shiny ribbon for her hair; just to see her smile and catch a breeze and gladly fly her a kite and keep it dancing in the air."

Q1198. "...For the names have all changed since you hung around, but those dreams have remained and they've turned around. Who'd of thought they'd lead ya, back here where we need ya..."

Q1199. "This is it, this is life, the one you get, so go out and have a ball...so while you're here enjoy the view, keep on doing what you do; hold on tight, we'll muddle through _____."

Q1200. "It's fun to laugh at yourself, it's a tonic tried and true; it's fun to look at yourself as other people do. How's your sense of humor? There's a rumor laughter's on its way; smile, you're on _____."

Q1201. "Yippie-i-o-ki-a, galloping all the way, great big star on his chest, outdraws all of the rest, fastest gun in the West."

A1194. *The Roaring 20s* (1960)

A1195. *The Double Life of Henry Phyfe* (1966)

A1196. *26 Men* (1957)

A1197. *The Sandy Duncan Show* (1972; a.k.a. *Funny Face*)

A1198. *Welcome Back, Kotter* (1975)

A1199. *One Day at a Time* (1975)

A1200. *Candid Camera* (1960)

A1201. *Quick Draw McGraw* (1959)

CHAPTER

8

Bonus Section

Identify the series by the excerpts of the TV themes listed below.

Q1.   "And there ain't no nothing we can't love each other through; what'll we do baby, without us."

Q2.   "Hello, world, here's a song that we're singing, come on get happy. A whole lot of lovin' is what we'll be bringing, we'll make you happy."

Q3.   "It's about two astronauts, it's about their fate, it's about a woman and her prehistoric mate. And now [name of show]."

Q4.   "Loving one who loves you and I'm taking that vow; nice work if you can get it and if you get it, won't you tell me how."

Q5.   "Where Indian fights are colorful sights and nobody takes a lickin'; where paleface and redskin both turn chicken."

Q6.   "He's a man of his word and the road he's chosen to follow brings him to this place and time; now he wears the badge—[name of show]."

Q7.   "He and she, you and me, the sweet blend of milk and honey, always together. We'll go through life discovering good things come in pairs."

Q8.   "Still they're cousins, identical cousins, and you'll find they laugh alike, they walk alike, at times they even talk alike; you can lose your mind when cousins are two of a kind."

A1.   *Family Ties* (1982)

A2.   *The Partridge Family* (1972 theme)

A3.   *It's About Time* (1966)

A4.   *Cybill* (1995)

A5.   *F Troop* (1965)

A6.   *Nashville 99* (1977)

A7.   *The Dumplings* (1976)

A8.   *The Patty Duke Show* (1963)

Q9. "You'll see him smile, right from the start, he'll play it smart. Beware of [name of show], he's such a lover, you'll discover when he steals your heart."

Q10. "We're tiny, we're tooney, we're all a little looney, and in this cartoonie we're invading your TV."

Q11. "Come on now and meet everybody and hear us singing. There is nothing better than being together when we're singing."

Q12. "I'm a good guy; hey, you're another one too. Like a brother, each to the other one true blue."

Q13. "She was a grandma to this lad, he was the son she never had, and together they hit the trail for Cal-i-forny."

Q14. "Girls, girls, girls, don't you wanna love 'em...some made of sugar, some made of spice, all made of everything that's nice, girls, girls, girls."

Q15. "I'm gonna make it forever, light up the sky like a flame...I want to live forever, baby remember my name, [name of show]."

Q16. "Take me home to the land of the Pecos, hear that stream, let me dream 'neath the sky..."

Q17. "Welcome to a land that's way under Down Under; the sky's always yellow in rain or shine..."

Q18. "I wanna happy ending, I'm tired of pretending, won't let 'em get the best of me. [name of show], the game is survival...and plan my arrival [name of show]."

Q19. "She's fantastic, made of plastic, microchips here and there; she's a [name of show] and brings love and laughter everywhere."

Q20. "In the eyes of a ranger, the unsuspecting stranger had better know the truth of wrong from right. 'Cause the eyes of the ranger are upon you."

A9.   *Flipper* (1967 theme)

A10.   *Tiny Toon Adventures* (1990)

A11.   *The Partridge Family* (1970 theme)

A12.   *The Good Guys* (1968)

A13.   *Dirty Sally* (1974)

A14.   *Sugar Time* (1977)

A15.   *Fame* (1982)

A16.   *Judge Roy Bean* (1955)

A17.   *Tazmania* (1993)

A18.   *Gimme a Break* (1981)

A19.   *Small Wonder* (1985)

A20.   *Walker, Texas Ranger* (1995 theme)

Q21. "Whenever I think of yesterday, I close my eyes and see that place just over the [name of show], that will always be home to me."

Q22. "He was a bold adventurin' man...his blade was tempered and so was he, indestructible steel was he...he was a fighter, a fearless, a mighty adventurin' man."

Q23. "There's a little hotel called the Shady Rest at the junction...it is run by Kate, come and be her guest at the junction...[name of show]"

Q24. "Yes, he's only a man, and he walks like a man along a path full of hills to climb without pause, climb them because he's a man."

Q25. "Bigger than big, taller than tall, quicker than quick, stronger than strong, ready to fight for right against wrong."

Q26. "I'm not the kind to kiss and tell but I've been seen with Farrah...I've gotten burned over Cheryl Tiegs, blown up for Raquel Welch...I'm the unknown stuntman who makes Eastwood look so fine."

Q27. "It's a grand life, it's an I've-got-the-world-in-my-hand life. It's an almost-more-than-you-can-stand life; strike up the band, it's a grand life."

Q28. "Thank God there is someone to pick up the phone, be my cornerstone; I'm not alone, thank God for a friend like you."

Q29. "You're never too old for love; never say no to love. Until the twilight comes, we'll take what time allows."

Q30. "How do I fit in, in a room full of women when they don't even know I exist? Daily I rehearse 'Ladies first,' 'Up with women'; still I'm at the bottom of the list."

Q31. "If I'm crazy, then it's true, and it's all because of you...but it just may be a lunatic you're looking for..."

Q32. "You couldn't call him pretty, yet you'd have to say he's kind of witty. Joey, Joey, Joey."

A21. *Brooklyn Bridge* (1992)

A22. *The Adventures of Jim Bowie* (1956)

A23. *Petticoat Junction* (1963)

A24. *Headmaster* (1970)

A25. *Gigantor* (1966)

A26. *The Fall Guy* (1981)

A27. *Marblehead Manor* (1987)

A28. *Hope and Gloria* (1995)

A29. *A Touch of Grace* (1973)

A30. *Ladies' Man* (1981)

A31. *Dave's World* (1993)

A32. *The Joey Bishop Show* (1962 theme)

Q33. "He protects and he saves his friends under the sea, that's where you'll find [name of show]."

Q34. "It's a rare condition in this day and age to read any good news on the newspaper page; and love and tradition of the grand desire, some people say is even harder to find..."

Q35. "She was working in a bridal shop in Flushing, Queens, till her boyfriend kicked her out in one of those crushing scenes; what was she to do, where was she to go, she was out on her fanny..."

Q36. "Hit the road, Jack, don't you come back no more, no more, no more! Hit the road, Jack, and don't you come back no more..."

Q37. "Thank you for being a friend, traveling down the road and back again. Your heart is true, you're a pal and a confidante."

Q38. "Everywhere you look there's a heart, a hand to hold on to...When you're lost...and all alone, a child is waitin' to carry you home, everywhere you look."

Q39. "The dream got broken, seemed like all was lost; what would be the future, could you pay the cost? You wonder will there ever be a second time around."

Q40. "Life goes on and so do we; just how we do it is no mystery. One by one we fill the days; we find a thousand different ways..."

Q41. "Standing tall on the wings of my dreams; rise and fall on the wings of my dreams...My life, my dreams, nothing's gonna stop me now."

Q42. "According to our new arrival, life is more than mere survival and we just might live the good life yet."

Q43. "Life is a riddle and you're in the middle and the puzzle is how to survive. Well you keep a-hopin' and you keep a-copin' and the answer will come to you [name of show]."

A33. *Diver Dan* (1960)

A34. *Family Matters* (1989)

A35. *The Nanny* (1993)

A36. *Unhappily Ever After* (1995)

A37. *The Golden Girls* (1985)

A38. *Full House* (1983)

A39. *Step by Step* (1991)

A40. *Empty Nest* (1988)

A41. *Perfect Strangers* (1986)

A42. *Mr. Belvedere* (1985)

A43. *Out of the Blue* (1979)

Q44. "There is a path you take and a path not taken, the choice is up to you my friend. Nights are long but you might awaken to a brand new life around the bend."

Q45. "If the teacher pops a test I know I'm in a mess and my dog ate all my homework last night...if I can hand it in tomorrow it'll be all right...'cause I'm [name of show]."

Q46. "Life goes on, right or wrong; now it's all been said and done...seems we've sung love's last song, poor John, seems we've sung love's last song."

Q47. "We've got laughs from coast to coast to make you smile, a real bright look at each of you...it's the honest things you do, America laughs at you."

Q48. "There's no place like home, with your family around, you're never alone. When you know you're loved, you don't need to roam because there's no place like home."

Q49. "Your friends will be there when your back is to the wall; you'll find you need us 'cause there's no one else to call...You better be ready to, be ready to jump [name of show]."

Q50. "...an angel on a visit to his brother here below can cause a lot of trouble; there's miracles from the start, but they always come apart on ...."

Q51. "I don't know, I don't care, I just got to be there. California, here I am and I love you; I've got the fever for you, fever, fever, fever."

Q52. "There's a hurricane a blowin' in over the water, waitin' in anticipation for the action to begin."

Q53. "Look right down any crowded hall you'll see there is a beauty standing; is she really everywhere or a reflection...could there be two different girls who look the same at [name of show]."

Q54. "Show me that smile again...don't waste another minute on your crying, we're nowhere near the end, the best is ready to begin."

A44.   *Who's the Boss?* (1984)

A45.   *Saved by the Bell* (1989)

A46.   *Dear John* (1988)

A47.   *America's Funniest Home Videos* (1993 theme)

A48.   *227* (1985)

A49.   *21 Jump Street* (1987)

A50.   *The Smothers Brothers Show* (1965)

A51.   *California Fever* (1979)

A52.   *Thunder in Paradise* (1994)

A53.   *Sweet Valley High* (1994)

A54.   *Growing Pains* (1985)

Q55. "Where is the best defense against the rising tide of crime? Where is the man who gives the law his heartiest support? I'll tell you where, it's [name of show]."

Q56. "You'll never guess [name of show] who's on the inside hanging out...sometimes this double life gets out of hand, but it's all in a day's work for Ultra Man."

Q57. "It's hard to lick the U.S. government; they're taxin' us and takin' every cent. The money comes and goes and we're paying through the nose..."

Q58. "It was you...you made me leap without taking a look; I never thought forever was the best I could do. Then came you, it was you and me and you, and then came you."

Q59. "Little bones and little hearts can sometimes end up broken; medicine works twice as well with understanding...Just give them love, a little love because tomorrow depends on [name of show]."

Q60. "When you're at the top, you've got it made...don't be afraid; when a chance comes along you must take it. You'll go far; the world's gonna know who you are..."

Q61. "So come along, my barefoot love, you can be that child of three as we laugh and play all the way knee deep in daisies with you."

Q62. "Don't go to bed with no price on your head...don't do the crime if you can't do the time..."

Q63. "Hey there, there's a world where we don't have to run...living free in harmony and majesty. Take me home, take me home."

Q64. "He stands for justice, he has no fears; he's the agent they call when trouble is near."

Q65. "Fame and fortune waiting to be won...a smile in the limelight and a place in the sun. I want it all, I want it all."

A55. *Sirota's Court* (1976)

A56. *My Secret Identity* (1988)

A57. *The Kallikaks* (1977)

A58. *Webster* (1983)

A59. *The Little People* (1972)

A60. *A Year at the Top* (1977)

A61. *Barefoot in the Park* (1970)

A62. *Baretta* (1975)

A63. *The Life and Times of Grizzly Adams* (1977)

A64. *Lancelot Link, Secret Chimp* (1970)

A65. *Blansky's Beauties* (1977)

Q66. "Here comes Sabrina, and all your friends are here again with you; and with Sabrina, there's fun and magic to keep you laughing too."

Q67. "Virginia, Virginia, Virginia, there's always something new in everything you do. Virginia, Virginia, Virginia, you've got a winning point of view."

Q68. "Love is crazy, it's unwise, it can take you by surprise."

Q69. "Archie's here, Betty's here, Veronica too. Reggie's here, and here comes Jughead and Hot Dog too, so everything's Archie; come on let's go with [name of show]."

Q70. "It's in the air, it's everywhere, people really startin' to care; they're gettin' [name of show]."

Q71. "Goin' down that long lonesome highway, gonna live life my way."

Q72. "Once before we took a chance and even though it didn't last [name of show]. Even though we share one life with your ex-husband and my ex-wife [name of show]."

Q73. "You're my inspiration, days are never blue. After all is said and done, there is really only one [name of show], it's you."

Q74. "She's laughter, she's magic, she's mine. She's an angel and angels are few. So everything I've ever dared to dream has come true."

Q75. "There's a new boy in the neighborhood; lives downstairs and it's understood he's just here to take good care of me like he's part of the family."

Q76. "He's smart as a fox, he's strong as an ox, but he's soft as a teddy bear. If you're backed up against the wall, all you gotta do is call [name of show], that's the man."

Q77. "…'cause each day is what you make it, our hopes are riding high and it's better when you share it, but we'll never know until we try."

A66.   *Sabrina, the Teenage Witch* (1971)

A67.   *The Virginia Graham Show* (1970 theme)

A68.   *Bridget Loves Bernie* (1972)

A69.   *The Archie Show* (1969)

A70.   *Getting Together* (1971)

A71.   *Then Came Bronson* (1969)

A72.   *Here We Go Again* (1973)

A73.   *Margie* (1962)

A74.   *Nancy* (1970)

A75.   *Charles in Charge* (1984)

A76.   *Big Eddie* (1975)

A77.   *A New Kind of Family* (1979)

Q78. "Love is harmony, love is family, love is you and me...and here is where the love is...right here for us all."

Q79. "There is a man the legends tell who stands for what is right. Like Wyatt Earp, he never shrieks or cowers from a fight."

Q80. "If we're ever puzzled by the changing times, there's a plate of homemade wishes on the kitchen windowsill and [name of show] to fill our lives with love."

Q81. "We're in the air and everywhere, flying high, flying loose, flying free as a summer breeze...we're in the air and everywhere."

Q82. "When the world never seems to be living up to your dreams, it's time you started finding out what everything is all about. When the boys you use to hate you date, I guess you best investigate [name of show]."

Q83. "You talk to people all day for a living, but all those easy answers you are giving—are you really living your life that way? Portland is a long way from L.A."

846. "Here he comes, here comes [name of show], he's a demon and he's gonna be chasing after someone."

Q85. "If you're in doubt about angels being real, I can arrange to change any doubts you may feel. Wait until you see my [name of show], you'll want her for your valentine..."

Q86. "You don't have to be a Mia or Sophia, this is the year of the Tom; be the shapiest, ickiest [name of show]."

Q87. "At a party she's a stomper, a rock 'n' rollin' romper; everybody's glad she came, hey that's [name of show]."

Q88. "Who likes it hot, who's getting steamy, who snores a lot, who's feeling dreamy; who cuddles and coos, who's loaded with animal drives [name of show]."

Q89. "I'm solid gold, I've got the goods; they stand when I walk through the neighborhood...I've got the chance, I'm takin' it, this time in life I'm [name of show]."

A78.   *Shirley* (1979)

A79.   *The Misadventures of Sheriff Lobo* (1979)

A80.   *Eight Is Enough* (1977)

A81.   *The Bugaloos* (1970)

A82.   *The Facts of Life* (1979)

A83.   *Hello, Larry* (1979)

A84.   *Speed Racer* (1967)

A85.   *Gidget* (1965)

A86.   *The Ugliest Girl in Town* (1967)

A87.   *Karen* (1964)

A88.   *Husbands, Wives, and Lovers* (1978)

A89.   *Making It* (1979)

Q90.   "Mission impossible is what they called our plan...we could have used a miracle or two; never thought we'd see it through [name of show]."

Q91.   "Hey look at me, I'm ready to fly; I'm ten feet off the ground, bound for the clear blue sky."

Q92.   "Life is a game we're playing, let the game begin; love is the word we're saying, better let it in."

Q93.   "Here comes the daydream drifting down on you...follow the dream until you see where it's going; like a kid, you're gonna feel yourself growing."

Q94.   "School's out, summer's comin'...just can't imagine what the world would be without a West Coast woman gettin' next to me. School's out, summer's comin'..."

Q95.   "Come to Bongo Congo, meet the ruling king, good King Leonardo, how that king can swing."

Q96.   "It's just another day, it's up to you to make it special. So enjoy it friend, today could be the day to find that rainbow again."

Q97.   "Leavin' the city, taking a chance to do what we wanna do. [name of show] for something really new."

Q98.   "If you have you and me, here in this shining world, there will be dreams to dance and summers to sing...if you have you and me there will be love."

Q99.   Like magic he appears, a hero to save the day. And just when you think he's here for good, that's when he goes away. 'Cause it's [name of show], he's never gonna settle down..."

Q100.   "Let the times roll, let your love grow; let the rain shower, let the rose flower. Love it seeks, love it finds, love it conquers; love it finds, love it seeks, and love it finds."

Q101.   "Pick out a star and wish, crazy as it may seem. Don't be afraid to hope, don't be afraid to dream..."

A90.   *In the Beginning* (1978)

A91.   *The Waverly Wonders* (1978)

A92.   *The Harvey Korman Show* (1978)

A93.   *Who's Watching the Kids?* (1978)

A94.   *Richie Brockelman, Private Eye* (1978)

A95.   *The King and Odie Show* (1960)

A96.   *Another Day* (1978)

A97.   *Please Stand By* (1978)

A98.   *Julie Farr, M.D.* (1978)

A99.   *Here's Boomer* (1980)

A100.   *Angie* (1979)

A101.   *Sweepstakes* (1979)

CHAPTER

9

1996–1998 Series

Questions are based on programs broadcast on ABC, CBS, Fox, NBC, UPN (United Paramount Network), the WB (Warner Bros. Network) and in syndication. The syndicated and UPN series questions were prepared with the help of Jennifer Santarsiero.

ABC

Dharma and Greg

Q1202. Dharma Finkelstein and Greg Montgomery are a happily married couple who are total opposites. She is a bit wild and crazy; he is quiet and conservative. Greg is an assistant U.S. attorney for the Justice Department. Dharma has two jobs. What are they?

Q1203. Dharma has always had a fondness for animals. What was the name of the dog she had as a kid?

Q1204. Now, as an adult, Dharma has two dogs. One is an older canine named Stinky. When Stinky made his Bar Mitzvah, Dharma gave him his own dog (making him the only dog on TV to have his own dog). What did Dharma name Stinky's dog?

The Drew Carey Show

Q1205. As any viewer knows, Drew is employed as the personnel director of the Cleveland-based Winford-Lauder Department Store. What prior job did Drew hold?

Q1206. Drew has three best friends, Kate, Oswald, and Louis. Kate works at Winford-Lauder in the cosmetics department. What jobs do Oswald and Louis hold?

Dharma and Greg

A1202. Dharma trains dogs during the day and teaches yoga classes at night.

A1203. Doobie

A1204. Nunzio

The Drew Carey Show

A1205. He was a waiter at Antonio's Restaurant.

A1206. Oswald is a delivery man for Global Delivery; Louis works as a janitor at the Drug-Co Chemical Company.

The Drew Carey Show continued

Q1207. Drew and the gang hang out at the Warsaw Tavern where they sell their homemade coffee-beer brew called Buzz Beer. What is the company's slogan?

Q1208. Drew, Louis, and Oswald have been friends since high school. At that time they had a band. What did they call themselves?

Q1209. Working at Winford-Lauder seems to be a pleasant job for everyone but Drew. His cubicle is opposite Mimi's, who is the boss's secretary. Mimi wears outlandish makeup, has a wardrobe from who knows where, and a distinct dislike of Drew. This paragon of fashion (at least she thinks so) has a side job selling what product?

Ellen

Q1210. The series started out with a simple premise: a single woman living in L.A. who relies on the support of her single friends. It soon evolved into a story about a lesbian looking for love. When Ellen finally admitted her sexuality, who was the first girl she kissed?

Q1211. Ellen is thirty-two years old and first owned a store called Buy the Book. Her friend Joe ran the coffee-shop section of the store. When Ellen sold the business, Joe opened his own store. What did he call it?

Q1212. Ellen's best friends are Paige, Adam, and Audrey. Adam is a photographer; Audrey assists Ellen at the book store; and Paige, the friend closest to Ellen, holds a job at what film studio?

Q1213. The sugary-sweet Audrey is not embarrassed to admit that her heroine is Florence Henderson (for her role of Carol Brady on *The Brady Bunch*). Ellen thinks that's cute, but won't admit certain things about herself—like her middle name. What is it?

A1207. "The Working Man's Beer"

A1208. The Horndogs

A1209. Sally Mae Cosmetics

Ellen

A1210. Her best friend Paige

A1211. Hot Cup of Joe

A1212. Tri-Global Pictures

A1213. Inez

Grace Under Fire

Q1214. Grace Kelly is a thirty-five-year-old divorcée struggling to raise three children. She once had a serious drinking problem, but has now cleaned up her act. What was it that Grace says made her see the light and stop drinking?

Q1215. Although it was an unladylike job, Grace was employed at the CBD Oil Refinery. In last season's episodes, Grace lost that job, but soon went to work as a bookkeeper at what company?

Q1216. Grace's best friends are her neighbors Nadine and Wade Swoboda. Nadine is a bartender and Wade originally worked as a telephone company lineman. What job did he take shortly before the series ended?

Lois and Clark: The New Adventures of Superman

Q1217. Clark Kent, alias Superman, is a reporter for the Metropolis *Daily Planet,* which editor Perry White calls "The greatest newspaper in the world." The paper does, however, have competition. What is the *Planet*'s rival?

Q1218. Perry White exclaims "Lois Lane is the best damn investigative reporter I've ever seen." Lois contends that "I always get involved in my stories." Lois also has a bad habit—eating chocolate. Where does she go to "pig out," as she calls it?

Q1219. Clark attended Smallville High School. Lois, born in Metropolis, attended Metropolis High School. What nickname did Lois have at this time?

Q1220. When two evil sisters, Lucille and Nell, came to Metropolis to destroy Superman with a laser beam derived from red Kryptonite, the device backfired and transferred Superman's powers to Lois. With the newly acquired super powers, she donned a purple costume. What did she call herself?

Grace Under Fire

A1214. "I saw a big red dog jump out of my lingerie drawer."

A1215. The Reliance Construction Company

A1216. TV traffic reporter for KQMO, Channel 6

Lois and Clark: The New Adventures of Superman

A1217. The Metropolis *Star*

A1218. The Fudge Castle

A1219. "Lo Lo"

A1220. Ultra Woman

The Naked Truth

Q1221. This series was originally called *Wilde Again* and dealt with the adventures of Nora Wilde, a photographer for a gossip paper called the *Comet*. In later episodes, Nora became a reporter for a rag owned by Camilla Dane. Name the tabloid.

Q1222. Nicky Columbus is a photographer on the *Comet*. As a ten-year-old boy he was the star of a TV series about an orphan who is raised by a family of otters. His companion on that series, "Nick Nick," was supposedly played by a young Sharon Stone. What was the name of this mythical TV series?

Q1223. When Nora was assigned to do a photo layout on big-breasted striptease dancers, she decided to pose as one. Instead of stuffing her bra with tissues, Nora used something completely different. To get the bounce she wanted, what did she use?

Sabrina, the Teenage Witch

Q1224. Sabrina Spellman is a beautiful sixteen-year-old girl whom no one would ever suspect is a witch. She is trying to be an average girl, but relies on her still-developing powers to get her out of scrapes. She attends Westbridge High School and works on the school newspaper. Name the paper.

Q1225. In the 1970s, witches abused their powers and conjured up an abundance of name-brand jeans. A law was passed prohibiting this from happening again. What happens when Sabrina tries to conjure up M&M's and a Butterfinger candy bar?

Q1226. Sabrina is cared for by her aunts, Hilda and Zelda. Hilda is a fancier of fine music; Zelda is a science nut who loves to experiment. She is also on the Internet. What is her on-line name?

The Naked Truth

A1221. The *Inquisitor*

A1222. *Otterboy*

A1223. M&M's (the plain ones)

Sabrina, the Teenage Witch

A1224. The *Lantern*

A1225. She gets "N&N's" and a "Butterthumb"

A1226. Chem Kitten

CBS

Cybill

Q1227. Cybill Sheridan is a single mother with two daughters (Zoey and Rachel), two ex-husbands (Jeff and Ira), and a classy, martini-drinking best friend (Maryann). Cybill is, in her own words, "an aging actress who loses jobs to younger girls." She takes what jobs she can get. In addition to doing a commercial for a feminine product called Femgel, name one other commercial Cybill made.

Q1228. Although she complains about how the younger actresses only get roles because they are willing to appear nude, Cybill decides to give in and show her breasts in what mythical cable movie?

Q1229. Cybill's TV career dates back to the 1960s. She played the Lizard Woman in an episode of *Star Trek,* but made her debut as the husband's secretary on what sitcom?

Q1230. Cybill made a guest appearance on the actual TV series *Stories of the Highway Patrol* ("I was hit by a bus") and made a TV series that was so bad that it never aired in the United States. Those six episodes were sold to Russian television and became their number-one show for seven years. Name the show.

Q1231. Match the character played by Cybill with the TV series on which that character appeared.
1. Booty, the Big Butt Clown   a. *Life Forms*
2. Sara McCullen   b. *Julie in the Morning*
3. Cybill Sheridan (Herself)   c. *Major Milo*
4. Galaxy Girl   d. *Invincible Girl*

Q1232. Cybill caught the show business bug at a young age when her cousin, pig farmer Lyle Slocum, entered her in a contest and she won the title "Miss Pickled Pigs' Feet." Since then she has appeared in "the worst horror film ever made" (*Oliver Twisted*) and on the sexiest network TV series ever made, the *X Files* rip-off, *Life Forms.* While Cybill is the star, the actual "stars" are what?

Cybill

A1227. Can-Do Supermarkets; Fraumeister Beer; The Psychic Pals Network; Granny's Snack Cakes

A1228. *What She Did for Love*

A1229. *Family House*

A1230. *Island Cop*

A1231. 1 and c
2 and a
3 and b
4 and d

A1232. "My breasts and legs, which get more airtime than the rest of me"

Dellaventura

Q1233. "Expect the Unexpected" is the philosophy of Anthony Dellaventura, a tough New York–based private detective who will do what it takes to get the job done. He also charges a hefty price. What are his fees?

Q1234. Before becoming a private eye, Anthony was a cop with which Manhattan precinct for fifteen years?

Q1235. Anthony's clients are people who have nowhere else to turn. The cases are sometimes complicated and can cause one to take an occasional drink. What is Anthony's favorite drink?

Q1236. Dellaventura quit the force because "I wanted to do things my way. They wouldn't let me." He loves happy endings and concludes each episode with what catchphrase?

The Nanny

Q1237. Before Fran Fine became the nanny to Broadway producer Maxwell Sheffield's three children (Maggie, Gracie, and Brighton) she worked at a bridal shop in Queens, N.Y. After three years she was fired and took a job selling what cosmetic door to door?

Q1238. Fran is now twenty-nine years old. As a kid she had a goldfish named Goldie, attended Flushing High School, and had her Sweet Sixteen party held at what establishment?

Q1239. Fran's favorite performer is Barbra Streisand. What possession of Barbra's does Fran own? (She paid $200 for it and had it framed.)

Q1240. Fran is an expert on 1960s TV shows and attended the Barbizon School of Modeling for two years (she was a foot model). What beauty school did she attend?

Q1241. When Fran appeared on *Jeopardy* (she won by $200 and became the champ) she was only the second person in her large family to ever appear on TV. Her cousin Ira was first. On what game show did he appear?

Dellaventura

A1233. $100 per hour, per associate

A1234. The 27th precinct

A1235. Root beer

A1236. "If you need me I'll be around."

The Nanny

A1237. Shades of the Orient

A1238. Benny's Clam Bar

A1239. A wad of bubble gum that came from the bottom of Barbra's shoe

A1240. The Ultissima Beauty Institute

A1241. *Queen for a Day*

The Nanny continued

Q1242. Gracie, the middle child, attends therapy sessions twice a week for being introverted and insecure. She is a member of the Red Robins scout troop, has a teddy bear she calls Mr. Fuzzy, and an imaginary friend. What is the name of her imaginary friend?

Nash Bridges

Q1243. Nash Bridges and his partner Joe Dominguez are detectives with the SIU Division of the San Francisco Police Department. What does SIU stand for?

Q1244. When an earthquake made the police headquarters building unsafe, operations were moved to the waterfront. What docked boat is now home to the SIU?

Q1245. Nash has a tendency to call everyone "Bubba," has a photographic memory, and loves magic. He also drives a rare 1970 yellow car of which only fourteen were made. Name the car.

Q1246. Nash carries badge number twenty-two and uses the above-described car as his squad car. What is his car code?

Touched by an Angel

Q1247. Tess and Monica are "visitors from Heaven who answer prayers." What position did Monica hold before she became a caseworker to help humans?

Q1248. While Tess has been an angel for some time, Monica is still a little wet behind the ears and likes to do things her way, sometimes angering higher powers. When is it that Monica wants to bend the rules?

Q1249. While angels apparently do not need to eat, Monica enjoys experimenting with new taste sensations. She is very fond of coffee and loves ice cream. What is Monica's favorite ice cream flavor?

A1242. Imogene

Nash Bridges

A1243. Special Investigative Unit

A1244. The *Eurika*

A1245. Plymouth Barracuda

A1246. 5-George-31

Touched by an Angel

A1247. Search and Rescue Angel (she was promoted when she saved a 747 plane)

A1248. "When my instincts kick in"

A1249. Java Jelly Bean Crunch

Fox

King of the Hill

Q1250. This animated series tells the story of Hank Hill, his wife, Peggy, their son, Bobby, and their niece, Lu Ann, all residents of Arlen, Texas. Hank is very proud of his job selling "propane and propane accessories" for Strickland Propane. What is the company's slogan?

Q1251. While Peggy does not work full time, she maintains her job as a teacher. She works as a substitute teaching what subject?

Q1252. When Hank and Peggy realized that Bobby was overweight and could no longer fit into clothes sold by Shelwyn's, they took him to another store where he went from wearing an extra large to a medium. What store was this?

Q1253. Hank and Peggy met at Arlen High School. While Bobby is not yet old enough to attend Arlen High, he does attend grammar school. Name the institution.

Living Single

Q1254. Khadijah, Regine, and Synclaire are three single women who share an apartment in Brooklyn, N.Y. Khadijah was the editor of both her high school and college newspapers and used that knowledge to start her own magazine called *Flavor.* Why does she call the magazine *Flavor?*

Q1255. Regine loves to shop, so she became a buyer for a boutique. She has to have a man at her side and shows lots of cleavage to attract men. She firmly believes in what she calls "The Three C's." What are they?

Q1256. Regine, whose real name is Regina, is on a mission to marry a man. She wants kids "because these genes are too good to waste" and believes she is irresistible to men. What occurs when the unthinkable happens and Regine has no man by her side?

King of the Hill

A1250. "Taste the meat, not the heat"

A1251. Spanish

A1252. H. Dumpty's

A1253. The Tom Landry Middle School

Living Single

A1254. "Because we've got taste and won't accept tasteless ads"

A1255. "Catch, Control, and Conquer"

A1256. She binges on chocolate.

Living Single continued

Q1257. Synclaire hails from Minneapolis and is Khadijah's cousin. She makes Christmas ornaments out of the eggs in which Leggs Pantyhose come and works as the receptionist for *Flavor.* She has a desk full of troll dolls to help spread joy and happiness in the office, but at the end of the day she is sad. Why?

Q1258. Overton Jones and Kyle Barker are the girls' upstairs neighbors and friends. Kyle is a stockbroker and Overton is a handyman. Overton is also Synclaire's boyfriend and lives by the handyman's oath. What is it?

Q1259. Overton has what he calls a "secret shame," a childhood fear that has followed him into adulthood. What is it?

The Mighty Morphin Power Rangers

Q1260. Jason, Trini, Zack, Kimberly, and Billy were the original Power Rangers, teenagers who fought the evil monsters of Rita Repulsa, an intergalactic sorceress bent on controlling the universe. Match the Power Ranger with the special Power Weapon he or she possesses.
1. Jason   a. Power Daggers
2. Kimberly   b. Power Sword
3. Trini   c. Power Lance
4. Billy   d. Power Ax
5. Zack   e. Power Bow

Q1261. Kimberly, the Pink Ranger, left the team to become a world class gymnast. Although she liked the Power Rangers costume, she hated the helmet. What did she say about it?

Q1262. Once they became Power Rangers, the teens took an oath to follow "The Code of the Power Rangers." What is this code?

A1257. Because she has to say goodbye to the makeup that got her through the day.

A1258. "I won't rest until it's fixed."

A1259. A fear of clowns

The Mighty Morphin Power Rangers

A1260. 1 and b
2 and e
3 and a
4 and c
5 and d

A1261. "The outfits are cool and everything, but my hair gets tangled up inside the helmet."

A1262. Never use your powers for personal gain; never escalate a battle unless Rita forces you; and keep your identity a secret

The Mighty Morphin Power Rangers *continued*

Q1263. When Rita and her successor, Lord Zedd, were defeated, another evil being, Price Sprockett, became a threat to the Earth. The series became "Power Rangers Zeo" and the new rangers were Catherine, Tanya, Rocky, Adam, and Tommy. Match the Power Ranger with his or her color costume.

1. Catherine	a. Yellow
2. Tanya	b. Green
3. Rocky	c. Red
4. Adam	d. Pink
5. Tommy	e. Blue

NBC

Caroline in the City

Q1264. Caroline Duffy is a cartoonist who draws the daily comic strip *Caroline in the City*. The strip is about a single girl who ventures into the city. When Caroline misses a deadline she becomes extremely upset. Why?

Q1265. As a ten-year-old, Caroline had a dog named Sparky and wanted something so bad that she drew them on everything. What did she want?

Q1266. When Caroline gets upset and has to have a drink, what is it that she must have? (It is the only thing that will calm her down.)

Q1267. Annie Spidaro, Caroline's sexy neighbor, is a professional dancer who performs in the Broadway play *Cats*. She also starred in a TV pilot that failed and did a commercial for what product?

Frasier

Q1268. Frasier Crane is a psychiatrist who hosts a daily call-in radio program on Seattle radio station KACL. What is its number on the AM dial?

A1263. 1 and d
2 and a
3 and e
4 and b
5 and c

Caroline in the City

A1264. When a "Caroline" strip is not ready, papers run two "Cathy" strips and Caroline hates the girl in those strips.

A1265. In her own words, "boobs"

A1266. Ginger ale

A1267. Dr. Furman's Foot Powder

Frasier

A1268. 780

Frasier continued

Q1269. Frasier lives in a luxurious apartment (number 1901) with his father, Martin, and Martin's live-in home-care specialist, Daphne Moon. What is the name of the apartment building?

Q1270. Although Martin is a retired cop, he is still trying to solve a twenty-year-old murder case of who killed a hooker and tried to stuff her body into a bowling-ball bag. What does he call this case?

Q1271. When Daphne was a girl in England, she was in a TV series about a twelve-year-old girl named Emma who lives in a boarding school. Name the show.

Q1272. When Frasier and his brother Niles learned that their favorite restaurant, Orsini's, was going out of business, they bought it and reopened it as what classy eatery?

Friends

Q1273. Rachel, Monica, Ross, Joey, Chandler, and Phoebe are the friends of the title. Joey is an aspiring actor whose big break came when he got the part of the "butt double" for Al Pacino in an unnamed movie. What agency represents Joey?

Q1274. When asked what her favorite movie is, Rachel will gladly tell you it's *Dangerous Liaisons*. But deep down she knows this is a lie. What is her favorite movie?

Q1275. Phoebe, the slightly dizzy blonde whom the friends call "Pheebs," is a folk singer and masseuse. She often sings at the friends' coffee-shop hangout, Central Perk; where does she work?

Q1276. Ross, who works at the Museum of Natural History, had an unusual pet—a monkey. What was his name?

Q1277. Monica works as a chef and appears to be the glue that holds the group together. But Monica also does silly things. The telephone pole outside her apartment house has something unusual on it. What did Monica put there?

A1269. **The Elliott Bay Towers**

A1270. **The Weeping Lotus Murder**

A1271. *Mind Your Knickers*

A1272. **The Happy Brothers Restaurant**

Friends

A1273. **The Estelle Leonard Talent Agency**

A1274. *Weekend at Bernie's*

A1275. **Healing Hands, Inc.**

A1276. **Marcel**

A1277. **Her bra**

Friends *continued*

Q1278. Chandler and Joey share an apartment. We know that Joey is an actor. What does Chandler do?

Just Shoot Me

Q1279. *Blush* is a New York–based fashion magazine owned by Jack Gallo. Jack is married to a girl thirty years his junior and says that his motto for running the magazine is the same as his blood type. What is it?

Q1280. Maya, Jack's daughter, is the articles editor for *Blush*. As a young girl she had an interest in flying and had a pet turtle. In college she majored in Shakespeare, appeared in ten productions, and had a pet cat. What did she name the turtle and the cat?

Q1281. Nina Van Horne was a top model of the 1970s and 1980s and is now the fashion editor. Because her real name was not sophisticated-sounding enough for a modeling career, she changed it. What is Nina's real name?

Q1282. Nina and Elliott, the fashion photographer, are friendly enemies who insult each other whenever possible. They do, however, have only one thing in common—a liking for a blues singer who recorded such "hits" as "A Pebble in My One Good Shoe," "Chin Hair Mama," and "Lazy Eyes, Swollen Glands." Who is he?

Something So Right

Q1283. Carly and Jack Farrell are a newlywed couple. Carly is twice divorced with two kids (Sarah and Will) and Jack is divorced with one child (Nicole). Jack works as a high school English teacher. What business does Carly run?

Q1284. Stephanie, Jack's gorgeous ex-wife, is the star of a TV series that got *Xena* star Lucy Lawless very angry. What is the rip-off series that Stephanie stars in?

Q1285. When Stephanie needed a daughter for her character, she chose Nicole to play Thora. This led to Nicole starring in a TV commercial. What product did Nicole sell?

A1278, He is a data processor.

Just Shoot Me

A1279. B-Positive

A1280. The turtle was Amelia Earhart; the cat, Othello.

A1281. Claire Noodleman

A1282. Cholera Joe Hopper

Something So Right

A1283. Get Down Tonight Party Planners

A1284. *Thena: Warrior Goddess*

A1285. Next to Nothing jeans

Suddenly Susan

Q1286. Brooke Shields is Susan Keane, a columnist for the San Francisco–based *Gate* magazine. Susan writes "Suddenly Susan." Exactly what is this column about?

Q1287. Vickie Groener writes about the hip scene and calls herself "The Empress of Hip." She also wears jersey No. 5 on an all-girl basketball team. What is the name of the team?

Q1288. Luis, the photographer, and Todd, the music critic, invested $1700 in a product for women—yellow bell-bottom pants. What did they call this company that failed?

Third Rock from the Sun

Q1289. Four male aliens are assigned to study Earth. They land near the Sweeney farm in Rutherford, Ohio, and adopt the aliases of Dick, Sally, Harry, and Tommy Solomon. Dick is their leader and acquires a job at Pendleton University teaching what subject?

Q1290. One alien lost the draw and had to become the woman. Sally, who is Dick's sister, is beautiful but is having a hard time adjusting to the female form. What does she call her breasts?

Q1291. Harry, the dimwitted member of the group, had an unexpected visit from his pet from the home planet. The lower life-form took on the appearance of a human, acted like a dog, and was named what?

Suddenly Susan

A1286. "Life and what happens to me"

A1287. The Vixens

Third Rock from the Sun

A1289. Quantum astrophysics

A1290. The Girls

A1291. Pickles

Syndicated

Baywatch Nights

Q1292. This spinoff from *Baywatch* began as a private-eye series dealing with the cases of Mitch Buchannon, Garner Ellerbee, and their beautiful partner, Ryan MacBride. It switched to a horror format during second-season episodes and soon disappeared. Although Mitch is a lifeguard on *Baywatch,* he always yearned to be a detective. When he was eight years old he saw what film that whetted his appetite?

Q1293. Mitch, Garner, and Ryan run the Buchannon-Ellerbee-MacBride Detective Agency. Ryan is also the firm's computer genius. What is the password for the office computer?

Q1294. Ryan is a former New York private investigator who actually owns the agency. It is located at 2000 Beach Blvd. in Santa Monica over what nightclub?

Conan: The Television Series

Q1295. Conan is a Cimmerian warrior who is following a destiny he does not understand (to become king—a prospect that angers Hissah Zul, an evil wizard who is seeking to destroy Conan so the wizard can become king). Conan has teamed with Otli, Zzben, and Biyou to fight the evils of Hissah Zul. What weapon does Conan possess that Hissah Zul fears?

Q1296. Hissah Zul rules the land from a mountaintop castle. He summons the Skull from a pool of water to "see" what is happening when he uses his magic to try to destroy Conan. What does Hissah Zul "pay" the Skull for its cooperation?

Q1297. Carella, a beautiful thief who calls herself "the Queen of Thieves" is also a warrior who suddenly appears to help Conan when he least expects it. Name the horse she rides.

Q1298. Speaking of horses, name the horse Biyou rides.

Baywatch Nights

A1292. *The Maltese Falcon*

A1293. Butthead

A1294. Nights

Conan: The Television Series

A1295. The Sword of Atlantis

A1296. Rubies

A1297. Indio

A1298. Thunderfoot

Hercules: The Legendary Journeys

Q1299. Hercules is the son of Zeus, the King of the Gods, and half-brother of Ares, the God of War. His stepmother is Hera, the all-powerful Queen of the Gods, who is seeking to destroy him. What was the first monster Hercules defeated?

Q1300. Iolaus is the warrior who travels with Hercules to help good defeat evil. Iolaus is two years older than Hercules. What did he do before joining Hercules?

Q1301. Although the marriage was short lived, Hercules wed Serena, a legendary creature who was half woman, half deer. What was she called?

Honey, I Shrunk the Kids

Q1302. This series, whose official title is *Disney's Honey I Shrunk the Kids, the TV Series,* is based on the movie series and deals with the wacky inventions of Wayne Szlinski. For what company does Wayne work?

Q1303. Wayne, his wife Diane, and their children Amy and Nick live in the town of Matheson. Their home is protected by a computer Wayne invented called FRAN. What does FRAN stand for?

Q1304. The family also has two pets, a hamster and a dog. The hamster is named Herkimer; what is the dog's name?

Q1305. Wayne has invented a number of things. His most famous is the Shrinking Ray. Which invention do Diane and the kids hate most?

Team Knight Rider

Q1306. *Team Knight Rider* is the series *Knight Rider* ten years later when it takes more than just one man (Michael Knight) to act on behalf of the Foundation for Law and Government. In the original series, Michael's roving headquarters was a black 18-wheel truck. Team Knight Rider uses a large cargo plane. What is it called?

Hercules: The Legendary Journeys

A1299. The snake in Ares' cavern

A1300. He was a master thief.

A1301. The Golden Hind

Honey, I Shrunk the Kids

A1302. Jentech West Labs

A1303. Felon Repeller Accident Neutralizer

A1304. Quark

A1305. The Igloo of Health (a plastic isolation bubble)

Team Knight Rider

A1306. Sky One

Team Knight Rider *continued*

Q1307. Kyle, Jenny, Erica, Trek, and Duke are Team Knight Rider. While Michael had KITT, each new member has his or her own vehicle. Match the team members with their cars.

1. Erica   a. Kat
2. Jenny   b. Beast
3. Kyle   c. Domino
4. Duke   d. Plato
5. Trek   e. Dante

Q1308. Trek, a computer genius, graduated from MIT at the age of ten; Kyle was a former CIA agent; what was Jenny's prior profession?

Q1309. "Who the heck would watch that show?" said Duke when he heard Jenny mention her favorite show as a kid. What real TV show was Jenny's favorite?

Xena: Warrior Princess

Q1310. Xena was originally an evil warrior who wanted to conquer Arcadia and become famous. She changed her ways when Hercules made her see herself as the murderer she had become. She and her traveling companion, Gabrielle, now fight to right wrongs. Xena has a weapon called a chakram (a circular piece of iron with sharp blades) and rides a horse. What is the name of the horse?

Q1311. In addition to playing Xena, Lucy Lawless played two Xena lookalikes, a harlot and a princess. Name either one.

Q1312. When Xena says "I smell burning" she knows her greatest enemy, Callisto, is about to appear to wreak havoc. Callisto has vowed to kill Xena because "years ago you barbecued my family." (Xena raided Callisto's village and an accidental fire destroyed it.) Despite their mutual hatred, they teamed to fight an evil Amazon—Xena to stop her; Callisto to acquire her Ambrosia, the food of the gods, which bestows immortality. Who was this Amazon?

A1307. 1 and a
       2 and c
       3 and e
       4 and b
       5 and d

A1308. She was a Marine.

A1309. *Josie and the Pussycats*

Xena: Warrior Princess

A1310. Argo

A1311. Meg the Harlot; Princess Diana

A1312. Velasca

Xena: Warrior Princess *continued*

Q1313. Shortly after the death of her husband Perdicus (killed by Callisto), Gabrielle is impregnated by the evil god Dayhawk. Gabrielle bears the child, a girl she later kills when she learns the child will destroy the world. What did Gabrielle name her daughter?

UPN

Clueless

Q1314. Cher Horowitz is a beautiful sixteen-year-old girl who lives at 2232 Karma Vista Drive in Beverly Hills. Her father is a wealthy lawyer and Cher attends a posh high school. Name the ultra-clean high school that even has a tanning salon for the students.

Q1315. Mel, Cher's father, deals with many show-business clients and is writing a novel, but never seems to have enough time to finish it. What is the title of his work in progress?

Q1316. Cher and her equally gorgeous girlfriend, Dee, are fashion conscious. What company did they form when Cher saw a picture of 1917 Russian women wearing muffs to keep their hands warm? (Hint: They combined the muff with a purse and named it after their two favorite movie stars—Brad Pitt and Keanu Reeves).

Q1317. Besides the tanning salon, Cher's high school has a basketball team mascot (most students didn't even know the school had a team, let alone a mascot). What is the mascot's name?

Q1318. When Cher needed to buy her father a birthday gift, she did the unthinkable—she went to the Valley and took a job as a salesgirl at a store to buy her father a present. Identify the store and the present.

A1313. Hope ("Because she was my hope")

Clueless

A1314. Bronson Alcott High School

A1315. *Hung Jury*

A1316. Brad-Keanu Muff Purse International, Inc.

A1317. Snappy, the Fighting Tortoise

A1318. The Valley Record Store; a Rain Forest Birthday Tree

Malcolm and Eddie

Q1319. Malcolm McGee and Eddie Sherman are buddies who share an apartment over a pub. Malcolm was an aspiring radio announcer when the series began and eventually gave that up when he bought the pub and changed the name to Malcolm McGee's Sports Bar. What was the original name of the pub?

Q1320. Eddie's Tow and Repair is the company run by Eddie. What does he call his tow truck?

Q1321. Malcolm and Eddie care about kids and coach a basketball team. What is the name of the team?

Star Trek: *Voyager*

Q1322. Kathryn Janeway, captain of the starship *Voyager*, considers her crew to be her family. Seven of Nine is one such member. She was an Earth girl who was assimilated into the evil Borg Collective. She was rescued by Kathryn and is now trying to become human again. On what starfleet spaceship had Seven of Nine been living when she was assimilated?

Q1323. The Borg are a Collective—a billion minds thinking as one. Seven of Nine was born on stardate 25479 and had been part of the Collective for twenty years. What is Seven of Nine's real name?

Q1324. Seven of Nine insists on absolute perfection. She is still a bit uneasy on *Voyager* and has a knack for upsetting Kathryn by disobeying orders. Where does Kathryn send Seven of Nine for punishment?

Q1325. Borg technology is extremely dangerous. Even one nanoprobe can spell disaster. Seven of Nine still carries those Nanoprobes as well as assimilation tubes in her arm. What is the implant over her left eyebrow called?

Q1326. When *Voyager* runs low on fuel Kathryn issues a Code Gray Alert (conserve energy) and uses a synthetic fuel until she can get the real thing. What is it?

Malcolm and Eddie

A1319. Kelly's Pub

A1320. Bronkula

A1321. The Little Dribblers

Star Trek: *Voyager*

A1322. The *Raven*

A1323. Annacha Hanson

A1324. The cargo bay

A1325. An occular implant (also called an electro optic implant)

A1326. Duterium

Sweet Valley High

Q1327. Elizabeth and Jessica Wakefield are gorgeous twins who attend Sweet Valley High School and who, according to Jessica, "share the same D.O.A." (of course, she means DNA). Jessica is obsessed with her body and beauty. Elizabeth is conservative and not as fashion conscious. Elizabeth yearns to be a journalist; Jessica would love to become a model or a movie star. Elizabeth works on the high school newspaper and interns at the local paper. Name both.

Q1328. Jessica also had an opportunity to make her dreams come true by appearing on TV twice. What commercial did she do with Elizabeth and on what show was she the cohost?

Q1329. Elizabeth's writing talents were finally realized when *Teen Lit* published her story "Platinum Blonde" (about a female spy whose code name was Double D 7). Jessica, on the other hand, has never read a book, let alone written one. But one day Elizabeth caught Jessica reading a book. It was a romantic novel Jessica just had to read. What book was it?

Q1330. While Jessica has, for the most part, rid herself of her childhood treasures, Elizabeth is a sentimentalist who hangs on to her childhood memories. Where does Elizabeth hide her money?

The WB

Buffy, the Vampire Slayer

Q1331. Buffy Summers is a sixteen-year-old girl who has become the Chosen One, a special girl who fights the demons of the underworld. An evil force known as the Hellmouth appears to be in the town of Sunnydale where Buffy attends Sunnydale High School. Buffy apparently has little time for school ("what with fighting vampires and such") and spends most of her time in the library helping her Watcher, Rupert Giles, research the demons she has to fight. What is Buffy's grade-point average?

Sweet Valley High

A1327. The *Oracle;* the *Tribune*

A1328. Nirvana Cosmetics; *Frankly Speaking*

A1329. *The Silos of Billings, Montana*

A1330. "In my Holly Hobby music box"

Buffy, the Vampire Slayer

A1331. 2.8

Buffy, the Vampire Slayer continued

Q1332. As a child, Buffy was fascinated with what sport (and what athlete was her hero)?

Q1333. There is a sadness in Buffy's eyes when she sees other girls doing the things she would like to do. In spite of all the trouble Buffy gets into, she did have a brief moment of glory at her prior high school in California. What was it?

Q1334. Cordellia Chase, the most popular girl at school, has her clothes specially made for her because "off-the-rack clothes give me the hives." She first thought Buffy and her friends (Willow and Zandor) were weird, but now helps Buffy in her quest. Cordellia also drives an expensive sports car. What does the license plate say?

7th Heaven

Q1335. Events in the lives of a minister, his wife, and their children are the basic premise of this series. Matt, Mary, Lucy, Simon, and Ruthie are the children; Eric and Annie, the parents; and, yes, there is a family dog. Name her.

Q1336. Eric is a passionate minister who takes a deep interest in the problems of his congregation. At what church does he preach?

Q1337. As a kid Eric attended Binghampton Elementary School. Match the Camden children with the schools they attend.
1. Ruthie   a. Walter Reed Jr. High School
2. Matt and Mary   b. Roosevelt Elementary School
3. Simon and Lucy c. Kennedy High School

Sister, Sister

Q1338. Twins separated at birth then reunited fourteen years later by a chance meeting at a mall forms the basis of this series. Tia and Tamera are the twins. Lisa and Ray are their adoptive parents. Who is the twins' birth mother?

A1332. Ice skating and Dorothy Hamill

A1333. She was voted May Queen

A1334. QUEEN C

7th Heaven

A1335. Happy

A1336. Glen Oak Community Church

A1337. 1 and b
        2 and c
        3 and a

Sister, Sister

A1338. Rachelle Gavin, an artist who gave them up at birth

Sister, Sister *continued*

Q1339. Tia and Tamera attend Roosevelt High School. Tia is the smart one and Tamera the one who does not apply herself. Tamera, however, is the school baseball team's star pitcher and winner of the school's first talent contest. Name the team and the title Tamera won.

Q1340. The twins first worked for Ray at his limo company. They then worked at what fast-food store?

Q1341. As a kid Tia had a favorite plush toy and Tamera a dog (which ran away from home). Name the toy and the dog.

Q1342. We know that Tia and Tamera attend Roosevelt High. What high schools did Lisa (Tia's mother) and Ray (Tamera's father) attend?

Q1343. Lisa is a fashion designer who uses her home as her one-woman factory. She sells her designs at a boutique called Monique's and in a cart at the mall that bears the name of her company. What is it?

Unhappily Ever After

Q1344. Jack and Jenny married young, had three kids, and separated. Jack went "crazy" and a plush rabbit known as Mr. Floppy came to life and helped Jack get his life together. A year later Jack moved back home (to the basement), got the wife and the kids, but has yet to find happiness. Jack has "affectionate" names for the kids (Ryan, Tiffany, and Ross). What are they?

Q1345. Ryan is the eldest child. He is extremely dimwitted and naive. Once, when struck by lightning (he hid in a metal garbage can during a thunder storm), he thought he was a super hero called Lightning Boy; and in a hairbrain scheme to make a million dollars, he started an Internet cyber sex service using (without her knowledge) Tiffany's name and picture. You could see Cyber Sex Tiffany by calling up what web site?

A1339. The Tigers; the Golden Casey Award (named after the school's most famous alumnus, Casey Kasem)

A1340. Rocket Burger

A1341. Mr. Froggy; Lulu

A1342. Ford High School (Lisa); Mumford High School (Ray)

A1343. Fashions by Lisa

Unhappily Ever After

A1344. The accident, the girl, and the mistake

A1345. www.tiffanymalloy.com

Unhappily Ever After *continued*

Q1346. Tiffany is a red-haired self-absorbed bombshell. She dresses extremely sexy "Because I love the power" and "I want to marry an old geezer who's loaded and has only a month to live." Tiffany has built her entire life around her physical beauty. Weighing herself makes her happy. What "teenage tragedy" befell Tiffany at the start of the second season?

Q1347. Tiffany is not always thinking of herself. "I collect money for the homeless so they can buy cheap wine," she says. When she thought she needed to be bad (to change her goody-two-shoes image), she shoplifted a lipstick, changed her name to "Toughany" and got a Popeye tattoo (the stick-on kind). This image lasted less than a day and she returned to the store to pay for the lipstick. Name the color of the lipstick she stole.

Q1348. In Jack's eyes, Tiffany can do no wrong. To get something from her father, Tiffany does "the pouty lips and Bambi eyes thing." To protect Tiffany from "the evils of boys and sex," Jack and Jenny show Tiffany a video tape that is "so horrendous" that even the home viewer was not permitted to see it. What is on this video tape?

Q1349. While only Jack and the audience can see that Mr. Floppy is "alive," Jack does find solace in talking to him. Mr. Floppy has this "thing" for Drew Barrymore, women's breasts, and a special doll. What doll does Mr. Floppy wish he could get his paws on again?

Q1350. When camera angles allow, kitchen shots often show the side of the refrigerator. One can see the Malloy's shopping list. What is the first item listed (and sometimes circled to make sure it is bought)?

A1346. She got her first (and only) zit. "Oh help me," she cried, "help me, I'm deformed."

A1347. Bad Girl Scarlet

A1348. Ryan's birth ("An ordeal no woman would ever want to go through," says Jenny)

A1349. Berbie (a takeoff on Barbie)

A1350. Beer